1000
ROMANTIC
THINGS
TO SAY AND DO

1000 ROMANTIC THINGS

TO SAY AND DO

ALICE STUART

MQP

An Hachette Livre Company
First Published in Great Britain in 2004 by MQ Publications,
a division of Octopus Publishing Group Ltd
2-4 Heron Quays
London E14 4JP

www.octopusbooks.co.uk

Copyright © Octopus Publishing Group Ltd, 2004, 2008

Text: Alice Stuart

ISBN: 978-1-84072-726-5
1 3 5 7 9 0 8 6 4

Printed and bound in China

CONTENTS

INTRODUCTION

What is romance? Is it diamond rings and boxes of truffles, or is it finding a note from your lover stuck to your computer when you sit down to work in the morning? Is it strolling along a beach at sunset, or is it abseiling down a cliff, roped together and hanging on for dear life? Romance means something different to everyone, which is why—when someone does something truly romantic just for you—it's so thrillingly, devastatingly effective. They have thought about you—what you might want, what you might like, what you might need—and then done everything necessary to provide it.

Some people wonder if romance is really necessary. Isn't it just the icing on the cake, the ribbon round the package? You love each other, right? Isn't that enough? Well, sure. Love's the most important thing. But isn't the icing what makes the cake delicious? Isn't the wrapping what makes the present exciting? And besides, what is love worth if you never show it? How will the person you love know? How will you?

A moment of romance in your day can make you feel alive, can remind you of what's most precious in your life, just when you were in danger of forgetting, or can let you know that someone's world revolves around you—even if you don't know who it is who's letting you know. The most fabulous thing about romance is that it doesn't have to be planned, it doesn't have to be big, it doesn't have to be expensive and you don't need to wear fancy clothes or book tickets to do it properly. Of course, romance can be all those things—and no doubt some of the most romantic moments in your life will come when you've put a little (or a lot!) of thought and effort into it. But romance can be something so tiny and insignificant—a squeeze of the hand, a look across a room— that it's barely noticeable to anyone else. In fact, those moments might be the essence of romance: meaningless to anyone else, but to the two of you, they mean the world.

"How on earth are you ever going to explain in terms of chemistry and physics so important a biological phenomenon as first love?"

Albert Einstein, scientist

YOU WON'T BELIEVE IT'S POSSIBLE, UNTIL IT HAPPENS TO YOU.

"I fell in love with my wife when I was 14 years old. People think that isn't possible, but fifty years later, there's never been anyone else who even came close."

Henry, retired teacher

You're never too old for your first love.

FIRST LOVE CAN STRIKE ANYWHERE. BE PREPARED.

11

"I thought I'd never love anyone as much as I loved James Dean. I was wrong, but it was a close-run thing."

Eileen, writer

YOU SHOULD ALWAYS LOVE LIKE YOU'VE NEVER BEEN HURT—THAT'S ONLY EASY THE FIRST TIME.

Once you have started falling in love, there is nothing you can do to stop it.

"I thought Adam was just a friend until the day he drove two hundred miles to comfort me after my dog died. It was then I realized I was wasting him on friendship."

Becca, designer

There is nothing in the world like a first kiss.

Love at first sight happens—so you might as well believe in it.

WHAT IS THE FEELING OF FIRST LOVE? IS IT BUTTERFLIES IN YOUR STOMACH...

...or goosebumps on your arms...

... or the blush on your cheeks...

...OR THE POUNDING OF YOUR HEART?

Young lovers have a lot
to teach their elders.

Smile at everyone you
meet—one of them might
be your soulmate.

"I remember being brought flowers when I was seventeen. I thought it was the most grown-up, romantic thing that had ever happened. They were probably picked from someone's garden."

Sophie, doctor

Your childhood only ends when you fall in love, because that's when the world stops revolving around you.

The sky will never be as blue as the day you first fall in love.

SOMEBODY THINKS ABOUT YOU ALL THE TIME, AND WISHES THEY COULD TELL YOU.

"The taste of cherry lipbalm, the smell of suntan lotion, and the sound of the sea all make me think of the first time I fell in love."

Patrick, software engineer

"I had been friends with her for years. One day we were talking, and she looked at me, laughing. And that was it—bam! I fell in love with her, just like that."

Nick, director

You're sure you are the first people on the planet ever to feel quite this way.

Falling in love means taking a great risk. It is, inevitably, worth it.

"Crushes are great—they give you a chance to practice for the real thing."

Amy, student

REMEMBER TAKING HOURS TO GET READY FOR EVERY DATE?

"When you fall in love for the first time you find out that all the stuff in films, in poetry, and songs . . . it's not made up."

Alex, investment analyst

"First love, with its frantic, haughty imagination, swings its object clear of the everyday, over the rut of living, making him all looks, silences, gestures, attitudes, a burning phrase with no context."

Elizabeth Bowen, novelist

The flush of first love might not last forever, but the memories of it will keep you together in years to come.

FIRST LOVE REQUIRES NO EFFORT, NO WORK, NO COMPROMISE. ENJOY THAT WHILE IT LASTS.

"I asked her to come for a walk on the beach with me, where I'd written, 'Will you be my girlfriend?' in pebbles. She said 'yes,' I'm pleased to report."

Simon, lawyer

NO ONE IS PERFECT, OF COURSE. BUT TO THIS PERSON, AT THIS TIME, YOU ARE.

"The first time a boy I liked called me up I was so excited I couldn't eat for two days."

Celia, human resources manager

Love is the
proof of the
existence
of God.

DON'T TELL YOURSELF YOU HAVE "A TYPE." THE PERSON YOU LOVE WON'T BE ANYTHING LIKE IT.

"I knew he loved me
when he offered to do
DIY for me. He doesn't
know one end of a drill
from the other."
Carla, hotel manager

YOU WILL NEVER BE THE SAME AGAIN.

Love really is "all around."

"Suddenly, it all made sense. I thought, 'So this is what I'm here for. To meet her.'"
Tom, accountant

"I WAS WITH SOMEONE ELSE, SOMEONE MUCH MORE SUITABLE, WHEN I MET HIM. BUT I JUST COULDN'T GET HIM OUT OF MY MIND, AND I'VE NEVER REGRETTED TAKING THE CHANCE."

ABI, MAKE-UP ARTIST

"I saw Viv on the other side of the room at a party I didn't even want to go to and I just knew, right then, that I was going to be with her forever."

Geoff, musician

Never keep love a secret. You never know who's dying to hear those words from you.

TRUE LOVE ISN'T TOO MUCH TO ASK.

Use the words "I love you" as often as you can. No one ever gets bored of hearing them.

"BEING IN LOVE IS LIKE GOING CRAZY. YOU CAN'T THINK STRAIGHT. AND YOU NEVER TOTALLY RECOVER."

PAUL, ENVIRONMENTAL ACTIVIST

Hopeless love, pointless love, ridiculous love—they have produced some of the happiest love stories of them all.

Test love to its limits.

"I went on holiday to Claire's hometown in the hope of running into her. My friends thought I was crazy. They were right, but now I'm married to her, I'm glad I did it."

Will, civil servant

LOVE MAKES EVERYTHING MAGICAL. JUST WALKING ALONG THE STREET AT NIGHT SEEMS LIKE THE MOST ROMANTIC THING THAT'S EVER HAPPENED.

You'll always remember your first kiss. Try to make your ninety-ninth as memorable.

> "I THOUGHT I HAD MY LIFE ENTIRELY FIGURED OUT UNTIL I MET HIM. AND THEN, IN ONE MOMENT, HE CHANGED EVERYTHING."
>
> CHERYL, EXAMINER

Sometimes you hear yourself saying "I love you" before you even realize you do. Don't worry. Your heart's just got tired of waiting for your head to catch up.

ALLOW YOURSELF TO BELIEVE THAT THINGS REALLY MIGHT BE AS GOOD AS THEY SEEM TO BE.

Don't wait, don't hesitate. Every moment
with someone you love is precious.

*Never be ashamed of falling
in love—it's the greatest
compliment you can
pay someone.*

On a first date, you're clumsy,
make bad jokes, and can't
think of anything interesting
to say. So how come they're
looking at you like they can't
wait for the second one?

"It was the weirdest feeling, like meeting someone you didn't realize you were waiting for. When we met, my first thought was, 'Oh, there you are.' "

Rachel, archivist

"The magic of first love is our ignorance that it can never end."

Benjamin Disraeli, 19th-century politician

SUDDENLY YOU ARE SOMEONE'S FAVORITE PERSON IN THE WHOLE WORLD.

DON'T MAKE THE MISTAKE OF THINKING THAT YOU'RE IN CONTROL OF LOVE.

Did the sun shine like this before? Did the birds sing like this before?

"Asking out a girl you really like is the worst feeling. It's almost enough to put you off doing it. Almost, but not quite. Because she might say 'yes,' and anything is worth that."

James, estate agent

Is the idea of falling in love any scarier than the idea of not?

"My childhood crush asked me to the school dance after years of me worshiping him from afar. I was walking on air for a week. When he kissed me, I swear I saw stars."

Kim, fashion buyer

"I USED TO THINK I'D GROW OUT OF THAT CHILDISH DAY-DREAMING, LOVE-SICK PHASE. HOW WRONG CAN YOU BE?"

THERESA, WEB DESIGNER

"When I knew that I would rather move to the other side of the world than be without her, that's pretty much when I knew I was in love."

Carl, biologist (now resident in Australia)

Nothing that lovers say to each other is original—
unless you're hearing it for the first time.

"The meeting of two personalities is like the contact of two chemical substances. If there is any reaction, both are transformed."

Carl Jung, psychologist

LOVE WILL CHANGE YOU. YOU CAN'T CHANGE BACK.

"True love is like ghosts, which everyone talks about and few have seen."

François, Duc de La Rochefoucauld, philanthropist and social reformer

You don't choose love. Love chooses you.

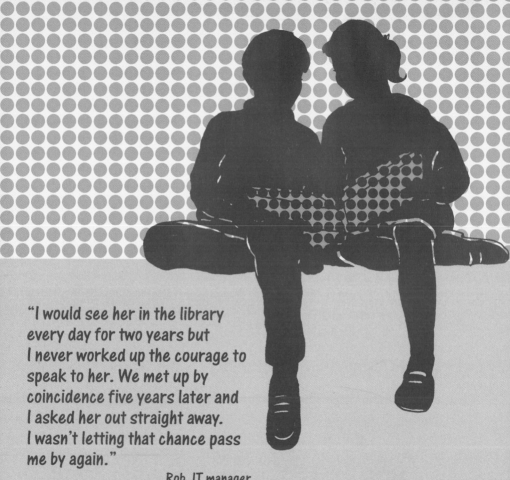

"I would see her in the library every day for two years but I never worked up the courage to speak to her. We met up by coincidence five years later and I asked her out straight away. I wasn't letting that chance pass me by again."

Rob, IT manager

LOVE CAN CREEP UP ON YOU, QUIETLY AND UNANNOUNCED. BY THE TIME YOU NOTICE, IT'S TOO LATE.

When the sound of a voice, a laugh can send you dizzy— that's first love.

Love and cynicism cannot coexist.

"The hunger for love is much more difficult to remove than the hunger for bread."

Mother Teresa

FIRST LOVE IS RECKLESS. YOU LEARN CAUTION LATER ON.

Do you imagine love won't happen to you? Oh really? What makes you so special that you'll be spared?

First dates can turn a local restaurant into the most perfect gastronomic experience of all time...

...and the cinema into an exotic palace of delights...

...though will you remember what film you saw...

"LOVE IS A SYMBOL OF ETERNITY. IT WIPES OUT ALL SENSE OF TIME, DESTROYING ALL MEMORY OF A BEGINNING AND ALL FEAR OF AN END."

ANONYMOUS

You might be sensible, you might be mature, you might be restrained. It doesn't matter—love will get you just the same.

Unrequited love is miserable, so you should check with the other person first—just to make sure.

First love is laughing at nothing.

BY REFUSING TO TAKE RISKS, YOU'RE GUARANTEED TO LOSE.

Believing in happy-ever-afters makes them more likely to come true.

"My first love happened when I was fourteen. I knew his school timetable off by heart, and I would 'accidentally' run into him about seventeen times a day."

Caroline, PA

"FIRST ROMANCE, FIRST LOVE, IS SOMETHING SO SPECIAL TO ALL OF US, BOTH EMOTIONALLY AND PHYSICALLY, THAT IT TOUCHES OUR LIVES AND ENRICHES THEM FOREVER."

ROSEMARY ROGERS, ROMANCE WRITER

When you fall in love, you will have the revelation that nothing in the world is as important as this.

"I knew he was the one for me when I couldn't stop smiling for a week. I haven't ever really stopped."

Emily, banker

THE ONLY WAY TO LEARN HOW TO LOVE IS TO PRACTICE.

Lovers can feel alone in a crowd, but never feel lonely.

"*Gravitation is not responsible for people falling in love.*"

Albert Einstein, scientist

LOVE WON'T ADAPT, SO YOU MIGHT HAVE TO.

Not everyone gets to feel this. No matter what, count yourself lucky.

You can fall in love many times, but first love only happens once.

"I ne'er was struck before that hour
With love so sudden and so sweet.
Her face it bloomed like a sweet flower
And stole my heart away complete."

John Clare, "First Love"

IF YOU DON'T BELIEVE IN DESTINY, LOVE MIGHT CHANGE YOUR MIND.

"We split up when we were eighteen because we thought maybe there was something better out there. We got back together when we were twenty-eight because we realized that there could never be."

Chris, sports therapist

"Love comes when manipulation stops; when you think more about the other person than about his or her reactions to you. When you dare to reveal yourself fully. When you dare to be vulnerable."

Dr. Joyce Brothers, T.V. psychologist

THERE ARE AS MANY DIFFERENT WAYS TO FALL IN LOVE AS THERE ARE PEOPLE TO FALL IN LOVE WITH.

"We don't believe in rheumatism or true love until after the first attack."

Marie Ebner Von Eschenbach, author

You can fall in love for an hour, a week, a year. . .or a lifetime.

"HE SAW ME THROUGH A MILLION ROTTEN DATES AND AWFUL BOYFRIENDS. ONE DAY HE SAID, 'WHAT ABOUT ME?' AND IT WAS LIKE THE LIGHT COMING ON."

TARA, ADVERTISING MANAGER

Everyone who falls in love acts like they're sixteen years old.

Don't expect people who've never been in love to understand.

"When love is not madness, it is not love."

Pedro Calderon de la Barca, dramatist

IF YOUR FIRST LOVE DOESN'T WORK OUT, DON'T IMAGINE YOU'LL NEVER FIND LOVE AGAIN. YOUR HEART HAS BEEN WEAKENED; IT'S SUSCEPTIBLE TO ANOTHER ATTACK.

Love is more than the sum of its parts.

> *"We were high school sweethearts and we met again after fifty years. Of course I couldn't expect it to be the same. But it was."*
> **Norma, grandmother**

63

There is an eternity of stars that you can have named for your loved one. Give them a little bit of heaven.

You know all those photos of each other that you keep taking? Find one you love, and get it enlarged and framed.

AN E-MAIL, JUST TO REMIND THEM THAT YOU LOVE THEM, MIGHT SEEM LIKE NOTHING TO YOU, BUT IT'S EVERYTHING TO THEM.

The words "You don't have to go to work today" may be the greatest sentence in the English language. Arrange a surprise day off for them with their boss.

GET A BACKCOPY OF THE NEWSPAPER FROM THE DAY YOU MET, EVEN THOUGH IT WON'T MENTION THE MOST IMPORTANT THING THAT HAPPENED THAT DAY—THEM.

Give them a back rub while you're watching TV.

Scour secondhand book shops for a first edition of their favorite book.

A plane ticket for the holiday of a lifetime . . .

. . . OR A SHELL FROM THE BEST BEACH YOU'VE EVER BEEN ON TOGETHER.

If you're web-literate, set up a website for them, telling them how much you love them.

A list of links to funny, cute, or interesting websites will help their day go faster and they'll think of you with every click.

CAN YOU BEAR IT? GIVE THEM A DAY (OR LONGER) OF FREEDOM FROM CHORES.

The personals column isn't just for Valentine's Day. Use it on any day of the year to tell them how much you love them.

Eating, taking a bath, going to bed—everything is more romantic done in candlelight; so scatter lit candles all around the house.

A book of love poetry is a classic gift. Tell them that every poem reminds you of them...

...OR MAKE YOUR OWN. PHOTOCOPY YOUR FAVORITE POEMS, OR PRINT THEM OUT FROM THE INTERNET; BIND THEM IN COLORED PAPER AND YOU'VE MADE THE BEST, MOST PERSONAL, ANTHOLOGY EVER.

Stock up the cupboards with their favorite food for them to find...

...or cook them their favorite meal.

Carnations are an eloquent flower for someone you are parted from. Send pink and it means "I'll never forget you;" striped means "I wish I could be with you" and red means "My heart aches for you."

A bouquet of beautiful flowers is the perfect romantic gift, be it from the most chic florist in town, or grown in your own greenhouse. Use the language of flowers to give your gift more meaning...

...ROSES HAVE MANY DIFFERENT MEANINGS. WHITE ROSES MEAN ETERNAL LOVE; PINK MEANS PERFECT HAPPINESS; A THORNLESS ROSE MEANS LOVE AT FIRST SIGHT AND RED ROSES—IN A BOUQUET OR A SINGLE STEM—SIMPLY MEAN "I LOVE YOU."

...CALLA OR ARUM LILIES INDICATE THE BEAUTY OF THE PERSON RECEIVING THEM; WHITE LILIES ARE FOR PURE LOVE. NEVER SEND ORANGE LILIES TO SOMEONE YOU LOVE—THEY MEAN HATE.

... iris would be the perfect gift for a long-term lover. They mean faith in your relationship, hope that it continues and give thanks for their wisdom and strength.

In general, tulips are the gift for a perfect lover. However, red tulips are a declaration of love, perfect for revealing yourself as a secret admirer.

Although its meaning is "hopeless love" you could consider sending some elegant sprays of dicentra. Its common English name is "bleeding heart" and rows of pink, heart-shaped flowers dangle from every stem.

Other flowers with romantic meanings include the vibrant dwarf sunflower, which means adoration; honeysuckle refers to the bond of love; and anemone indicates unfading love and affection.

IF YOUR OTHER HALF IS A SPORTS FAN, BUY THEM TICKETS FOR THE MATCH ... AND LET HIM TAKE SOMEONE WHO'LL ENJOY IT, EVEN IF THAT ISN'T YOU.

If they're running late for work, iron their shirt for them.

When you're out buying the newspapers, pick up a packet of Love Heart candies for them ...

One of the most precious gifts you can give is totally free: your time and your attention.

Just pick something up for them on your way home; it could be a leaf, a pretty card or a bottle of wine—just to say you were thinking about them.

SELECT A FAVORITE BOOK AND READ TO THEM.

If there's something of yours that they use all the time—a T-shirt they sleep in, a CD they listen to, or a book they love—wrap it up and hand it over, officially.

Making someone giggle makes you feel great. Laugh at their jokes!

Lingerie is a romantic classic. Make sure you pick something in their style and size . . .

. . . or buy some for yourself and unveil it. (This works even better if it's hiding under your old jumper and jeans.)

A packet of seeds means you can grow your own flowers or food together: It's amazing how attached you get to some little green shoots emerging from the earth.

Buy some original artwork so they can be surrounded by beautiful, individual objects...

...OR IF YOU FEEL UP TO IT, CREATE SOME YOURSELF.

Arrange for out-of-town friends or family to come and stay as a surprise.

80

Meet me at the airport. Bring your passport.
Where are we going?
That's up to you.

ON VALENTINE'S DAY
SEND THEM AN EXTRA
ANONYMOUS CARD.
EVERYONE FEELS GREAT
THINKING THEY HAVE
A SECRET ADMIRER.

Fix them a drink—
without them having to ask.

There's an outfit you know that they
love—even if you aren't so sure. Wear it.

Something—anything—made of silk or cashmere, to show that you think they deserve the best.

MAKE THEM A PACKED LUNCH TO TAKE TO WORK—AND MAKE SURE IT'S TOTALLY DELICIOUS.

"I love you" is great, but it's hardly specific. Are you thankful? Lustful? Amazed? Let them know, in words or writing. It's the kind of detail no one ever gets tired of.

Music is the food of love—and the soundtrack to your own personal romance. Compile a list of songs that you've danced, laughed, fought, and sung along to, then make a tape, a mini-disc, burn them on to a CD or download them onto their MP3 player.

Internet auctions are your best resource for the perfect "where-did-you-find-that?" present: A Star Wars figure; a 1930s coat; or a Victorian chaise longue.

Do they have a secret ambition? Buy paper for wannabe writers; paints for closet artists; or recording equipment for bedroom musicians. It shows you believe in them and what they can be.

TELL A LIE FOR THEM. EVEN IF IT'S JUST TELLING THEIR BOSS, "NO, THEY'RE REALLY ILL—THERE'S NO WAY THEY CAN COME TO WORK TODAY," AS THEY LOAD UP THE CAR FOR A DAY TRIP.

SURRENDER ONE OF YOUR BABY PICTURES. IT'S CUTE, IT'S FUNNY AND—LET'S FACE IT—IT MEANS YOUR MOTHER CAN'T EMBARRASS YOU BY SHOWING THEM OFF.

Even if they've only been over the road to get some milk, greet them with a passionate embrace.

A bottle of champagne. It works in the swankiest bar in town, or with oysters at the best restaurant . . .

. . . AND SOMEHOW EVEN BETTER OUT OF PLASTIC CUPS, WITH A BAG OF FRENCH FRIES, SITTING ON A BENCH BY THE RIVER.

If they're not in the habit of being extravagant, buy them something they'd never dream of getting for themselves...

...OR, IF THEY ARE, BITE YOUR TONGUE AS THEY HEAD TO THE CASH DESK, RATHER THAN YELLING, "HOW MUCH?!" AT THEM ALL THE WAY HOME.

A subscription to their favorite magazine reminds them of you every time it arrives.

Bring them breakfast in bed—and don't worry about the crumbs.

IF YOU SORT OUT SOME TIDYING OR DIY WHILE THEY'RE AWAY, THEY'LL LOVE THAT IT'S DONE AND, EVEN MORE, THEY'LL LOVE THAT THEY DIDN'T HAVE TO DO IT THEMSELVES.

Do they love burning rubber?
Arrange a test drive for their dream
car. Let them wear shades and pose
as if they owned it.

If you're a millionaire, buy them a house.
Failing that, draw them a picture of the
house you want to live in one day, with them.

Make them a cake, then ice
their name on the top. It's
essential that it's a bit wobbly,
for that homespun feel.

With some care and attention, a tree will burst into new life and grow stronger and bigger every year. Hopefully, your relationship will do the same. And in years to come you can sit in its shade and watch the blossom fall.

No matter what they (and the neighbors) might think—you really don't mind their morning sing-a-long. Buy them a shower radio to prove it.

Do they wear perfume or aftershave? Buy them a bottle of their favorite...

...OR IF YOU DO, GIVE THEM SOMETHING THAT SMELLS OF IT. SMELL IS THE MOST POWERFUL SENSE AND WHEN YOU'RE APART THEY WILL BE ABLE TO CLOSE THEIR EYES AND CONJURE YOU UP.

IT MIGHT ALMOST KILL YOU TO DO IT ... BUT LET THEM WIN AN ARGUMENT.

Have doughnuts and coffee delivered to their office—or drop them off yourself.

If you can't afford a vacation right now, buy a travel guide so at least you can plan where you'll go together.

Why don't you write them a poem? It needn't be long, or corny—only sincere. It'll be the best thing they've ever read, no matter what it says.

Sneakily set the alarm clock for an hour earlier so you can share some time together—no one's saying you have to get out of bed.

If you don't live together, give them a drawer for their stuff at your house.

SO IT'S A LITTLE BIT OBVIOUS, BUT IF YOU SCATTER ROSE PETALS ON THEIR BED NO ONE COULD DOUBT WHAT YOU WERE TRYING TO SAY.

Get technical and set up the desktop and screensaver on their computer to display a special picture or just **"I love you."**

What's their passion? Pay for them to do an evening class in it.

Save them the commute home and pick them up from work in your car.

Tell them a secret about yourself.

SOMETIMES IT CAN BE HARD TO SAY THINGS FACE-TO-FACE, SO LET YOUR FEELINGS FLOW IN A LOVE LETTER.

Tell them "I love you," in English . . .

. . . or "Je t'aime," in French . . .

. . . or "Ich liebe dich," in German . . .

...or "Ti amo," in Italian...

...OR "TE AMO," IN SPANISH...

...or why not try "Ngiyakuthanda!" in Zulu; "Techihhila" in Sioux; "Mai tumse pyar karta hoo" in Hindi; "Mi amas vin" in Esperanto; or "Wani ra yana ro aisha" in Vulcan, for the Star Trek fans among you.

DOES YOUR LOCAL RADIO STATION DO REQUESTS? PHONE IN AND DEDICATE A SONG TO THEM. ONLY MAKE SURE THEY'RE LISTENING.

There must be something neither of you have ever done before. Try it. You might love it, and if you hate it you'll hate it together.

The definition of real love: Letting them have control of the car stereo on a long journey.

Run them a bath. Don't forget the bubbles.

The very first flowers from the garden left in a jar by the bed. Around Valentine's Day you'll find perfect narcissi, shy hellebores, and jewel-like crocuses.

Challenge them to a board game championship and provide Trivial Pursuits, Monopoly, or Jenga. If you're feeling really generous, you could let them win. Once.

IF YOU CAN'T BE TOGETHER FOR A WHILE, TELL THEM YOU LOVE THEM ON VIDEO THEN MAIL IT TO THEM.

No one ever gets bored of hearing that they look nice, so pay them a compliment.

Instead of a card, send an origami creation. The thought of you frowning over getting the folds right will be enough to make them smile for the rest of the day.

Buy a cook book and promise to make the meal of their choice from it. Keep the promise!

Do they love their bed? Get them luxurious new linen (and make their bed up for them.)

IN A DIARY, WRITE ON EVERY PAGE SOMETHING THAT YOU LOVE ABOUT THE PERSON YOU'RE GIVING IT TO. IT WILL MAKE THEM FEEL SPECIAL EVERY DAY.

You never want any rain to fall in their life. Give them an umbrella.

Plan dates and events for the two of you to fill the next six months. Give them a calendar with them all marked.

HOW ABOUT A BOX OF THE MOST EXQUISITE, REFINED, HANDCRAFTED CHOCOLATES YOU CAN FIND...

... or a bag of M&Ms? Both say, "I think you're sweet, and you don't need to diet."

BUY THEM THAT PUPPY (OR KITTEN, OR RABBIT ...) THAT THEY'VE ALWAYS WANTED. THEN HELP THEM LOOK AFTER IT.

Found a four leafed clover? Give it to them. If you haven't, maybe a lucky horseshoe would do instead?

Get up early to make their first cup of coffee in the coffee pot, rather than letting them drink instant.

It's the ultimate luxury: Arrange for them to have a piece of clothing handmade just for them.

IF THEY'RE SCARED OF BUGS, BUY THEM BUG SPRAY AND A SPIDER TRAP. OR PROMISE TO ALWAYS DEAL WITH CREEPY CRAWLIES YOURSELF.

Two webcams will mean you can talk online to each other no matter where you are.

A POSY OF WILD FLOWERS PICKED THAT MORNING— AND IT MEANS EVEN MORE IF YOU LIVE IN THE CITY.

Hunt down an autograph from their favorite celebrity.

RECEIVING AN E-CARD AT WORK IS SO MUCH NICER THAN CHECKING LAST YEAR'S SALES FIGURES.

There's nothing nicer than the smell of baking wafting through your house. Make them some bread (or if they've got a sweet tooth, some cookies).

Paired up with a film buff? Get them a copy of their favorite movie on DVD, then promise to watch it with them. Even if you hate it. Especially if you hate it.

Take them out for the evening—and tape their favorite TV program so you can watch it when you come home.

Buy them a bed—for you to share.

GET CRAFTY: FIND A BORING BOOK, STICK THE PAGES TOGETHER, CUT A HOLE IN THE MIDDLE AND HIDE A GIFT THEY REALLY WANT INSIDE.

INTERNET SHOPPING IS A MARVELOUS THING: ARRANGE TO HAVE THEIR GROCERY SHOPPING DELIVERED AT HOME.

A massage is the perfect gift for the stressed-out person in your life. Or, if you prefer, administer it yourself.

Get a T-shirt printed with a picture of yourself or an in-joke on it.

Be industrious and leave love notes everywhere they'll find them—the bathroom mirror, the fridge, the car, their glasses case.

TWO MINUTES OF SILLY POSING TOGETHER IN A PHOTO BOOTH AND YOU GET A STRIP OF MEMORIES TO MAKE YOU SMILE FOREVER.

You can't say no: Give them tokens for favors they can demand of you—any time they like it. It could be doing the washing up, or heading for an early night . . .

GIVE YOUR HEART. IT'S THE EASIEST AND HARDEST THING YOU CAN DO.

"Other men said they have seen angels,
But I have seen thee
and thou art enough."

George Moore

"I love you—those three words have my life in them."

Alexandrea to Nicholas III

"WHAT LIES BEHIND US, AND WHAT LIES BEFORE US ARE TINY MATTERS COMPARED TO WHAT LIES WITHIN US."

RALPH WALDO EMERSON

"I HAVE BEEN ASTONISHED THAT
MEN COULD DIE MARTYRS FOR THEIR
RELIGION—I HAVE SHUDDER'D AT IT.
I SHUDDER NO MORE.
I COULD BE MARTYR'D FOR MY
RELIGION—LOVE IS MY RELIGION—
AND I COULD DIE FOR THAT.
I COULD DIE FOR YOU."

JOHN KEATS

"I'd like to run away
From you,
But if you didn't come
And find me ...
I would die."

Shirley Bassey

"When you love someone, all your
saved-up wishes start coming out."

Elizabeth Bowen

"Soul meets soul on lovers' lips."

Percy Bysshe Shelley

"I LOVE THEE, I LOVE BUT THEE
WITH A LOVE THAT SHALL NOT DIE
TILL THE SUN GROWS COLD
AND THE STARS GROW OLD."

WILLIAM SHAKESPEARE

"True love cannot be found
where it truly does not exist,
Nor can it be hidden where
it truly does."

Anonymous

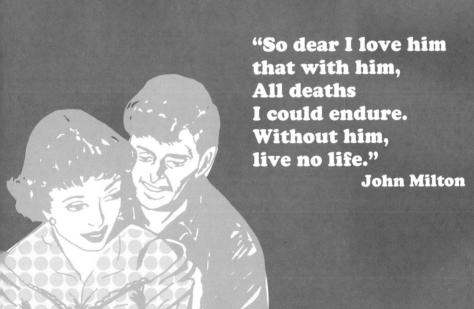

"To live is like to love—
all reason is against it,
and all healthy instinct for it."

Samuel Butler

"So dear I love him
that with him,
All deaths
I could endure.
Without him,
live no life."

John Milton

"I HAVE LOVED TO THE POINT OF MADNESS;
THAT WHICH IS CALLED MADNESS, THAT WHICH
TO ME, IS THE ONLY SENSIBLE WAY TO LOVE."
FRANÇOISE SAGAN

"One word frees us
Of all the weight
And pain in life,
That word is Love."
Sophocles

"LOVE IS LIKE WAR,
EASY TO BEGIN BUT HARD TO END."
ANONYMOUS

"I have learned not to worry about love;
But to honor its coming with all my heart."
Alice Walker

"A kiss is a lovely trick
designed by nature
To stop speech when words
become superfluous."
                    Ingrid Bergman

"GROW OLD ALONG WITH ME
THE BEST IS YET TO BE."
                    ROBERT BROWNING

"Love is patient, love is kind. It does not envy, it does not boast, it is not proud. It is not rude, it is not self-seeking, it is not easily angered, it keeps no record of wrongs. Love does not delight in evil but rejoices with the truth. It always protects, always trusts, always hopes, always perseveres."

The Bible: 1 Corinthians 13:4–7

"I love you not only for
what you are,
But for what I am when
I am with you."
Elizabeth Barrett Browning

"A Friend's love says:
'If you ever need anything,
I'll be there.'
True Love says:
'You'll never need anything;
I'll be there.' "

Jimi Hollemans

**"LOVE IS FRIENDSHIP
SET ON FIRE."**
JEREMY TAYLOR

"WHAT A GRAND THING, TO BE LOVED! WHAT A GRANDER THING STILL, TO LOVE!"

VICTOR HUGO

"Love is a fire. But whether it is going to warm your heart or burn down your house, you can never tell."

Joan Crawford

"I seem to have loved you in numberless forms, numberless times, in life after life, in age after age forever."

Rabindranath Tagore

"For one human being to love another: That is perhaps the most difficult of our tasks; the ultimate, the last test and proof, the work for which all other work is but preparation."

Rainer Maria Rilke

"WHO, BEING LOVED, IS POOR?"
OSCAR WILDE

"If you have it, you don't need to have anything else.
If you don't have it, it doesn't matter much what else you have."

James M. Barrie

"Love is like quicksilver
in the hand.
Leave the fingers
open and it stays.
Clutch it, and it darts away."

Dorothy Parker

"You were born together,
and together you shall be for evermore.
You shall be together when the white
wings of death scatter your days.
Aye, you shall be together even
in the silent memory of God.
But let there be spaces in your togetherness.
And let the winds of the heavens
dance between you."

Kahlil Gibran

"Love is a wound within the body
That has no outward sign."

Marie de France

"O Love, O fire! once he drew
With one long kiss my whole
soul through,
My lips, as sunlight drinketh dew."

Alfred, Lord Tennyson

"LOVE IS, ABOVE ALL, THE
GIFT OF ONESELF."

JEAN ANOUILH

"Love, and do what you like."

St. Augustine

"RISE UP, MY LOVE, MY FAIR ONE,
AND COME AWAY.
FOR, LO, THE WINTER IS PAST, THE
RAIN IS OVER AND GONE;
THE FLOWERS APPEAR ON THE EARTH;
THE TIME OF THE SINGING OF BIRDS IS
COME, AND THE VOICE OF THE TURTLE
IS HEARD IN OUR LAND."

THE BIBLE: SONG OF SOLOMON, 2:10

"I love thee to the depth and breadth
and height my soul can reach."

Elizabeth Barrett Browning

"THEY DO NOT LOVE THAT DO
NOT SHOW THEIR LOVE."
WILLIAM SHAKESPEARE

"I, being poor, have only my dreams;
I have spread my dreams under your feet;
Tread softly because you tread on my
dreams."

William Butler Yeats

"I wonder, by my troth,
what thou and I did,
till we lov'd?"

John Donne

"MY BOUNTY IS AS BOUNDLESS
AS THE SEA, MY LOVE AS DEEP;
THE MORE I GIVE TO THEE, THE
MORE I HAVE, FOR BOTH
ARE INFINITE."

WILLIAM SHAKESPEARE

"Two souls with but a single thought, two hearts that beat as one."

John Keats

"So long as men can breathe or eyes can see, so long lives this, and this gives life to thee."

William Shakespeare

"Don't say you love me unless you really mean it because I might do something crazy like believe it."

Anonymous

"Tis the most tender part of love, each other to forgive."

John Sheffield

"Doubt thou the stars are fire;
Doubt that the sun doth move;
Doubt truth to be a liar;
But never doubt I love."

William Shakespeare

"SOME PEOPLE COME INTO OUR LIVES, LEAVE FOOTPRINTS IN OUR HEARTS, AND WE ARE NEVER EVER THE SAME."

ANONYMOUS

"LET US NOT LOVE WITH WORDS OR TONGUE BUT WITH ACTIONS AND IN TRUTH."

THE BIBLE: 1 JOHN 3:18

"And if you ever decided to leave me I would go and find you and bring you home because you would be wrong."

Anonymous

"It is impossible to love and be wise."

Francis Bacon

"I COME HERE WITH NO EXPECTATIONS, ONLY TO PROFESS, NOW I AM AT THE LIBERTY TO DO SO, THAT MY HEART IS AND WILL ALWAYS BE YOURS."

JANE AUSTEN, SENSE AND SENSIBILITY

"Love is not love

Which alters when it alteration finds,

Or bends with the remover to remove.

O, no! It is an ever-fixed mark,

That looks on tempests and is never shaken."

William Shakespeare

"Who so loves believes the impossible."
Elizabeth Barrett Browning

"Your words are my food, your breath my wine. You are everything to me."

Sarah Bernhardt

"Among those whom I like or admire, I can find no common denominator, but among those whom I love, I can: all of them make me laugh."

W.H. Auden

"Never seek to tell thy love,
Love that never told can be;
For the gentle wind does move,
Silently, invisibly."

William Blake

"Love does not consist of gazing at each other,
but looking outward in the same direction."

Antoine de Saint-Exupéry

"We are all born for love. It
is the principle of existence,
and its only end."

Benjamin Disraeli

"NEVER CLOSE YOUR LIPS TO
THOSE TO WHOM YOU HAVE
OPENED YOUR HEART."

CHARLES DICKENS

"Only passions, great passions, can elevate the soul to great things."

Denis Diderot

"Love is the whole and more than all."
E.E. Cummings

"What greater thing is there for two human souls than to feel that they are joined together to strengthen each other in all labour, to minister to each other in all sorrow, to share with each other in all gladness, to be one with each other in the silent unspoken memories?"

George Eliot

"Love is an act of faith."

Erich Fromm

"TILL I LOVED I NEVER LIVED."

EMILY DICKINSON

"Your slightest look easily will unclose me, though I have closed myself as fingers, you open petal by petal myself as Spring opens her first rose."

E.E. Cummings

"I'VE LOOKED AROUND ENOUGH TO KNOW THAT YOU'RE THE ONE I WANT TO GO THROUGH TIME WITH."

JIM CROCE

"Where love is concerned, too much is not even enough."

P.A.C. de Beaumarchais

"Where there is great love,
there are always miracles."

Willa Cather

**"Love works in miracles every day:
Such as weakening the strong, and
stretching the weak; making fools of
the wise, and wise men of fools;
favoring the passions, destroying
reason, and in a word, turning
everything topsy-turvy."**

Marguerite de Valois

"It is love alone that gives
worth to all things."

Santa Teresa de Jésus

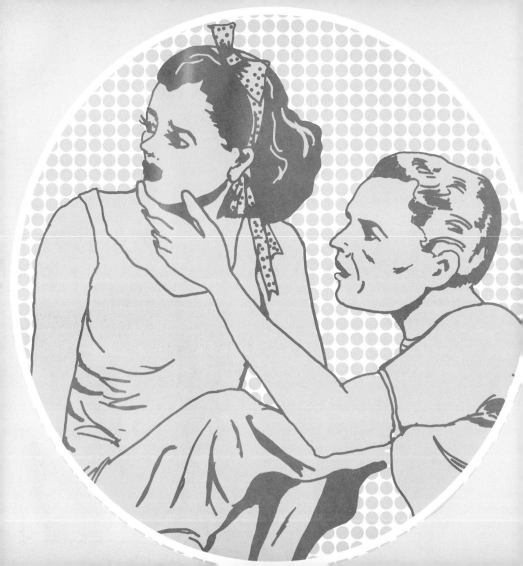

"LOVE IS WHEN REALITY IS BETTER THAN YOUR DREAMS."

BECKY GRAHAM

"Love is everything it's cracked up to be. That's why people are so cynical about it. It really is worth fighting for, being brave for, risking everything for. And the trouble is if you don't risk anything, you risk even more."

Erica Jong

"Love doesn't make the world go round.
Love is what makes the ride worthwhile."

Franklin P. Jones

"There is only one terminal dignity—love. And the story of a love is not important —what is important is that one is capable of love. It is perhaps the only glimpse we are permitted of eternity."

Helen Hayes

"Where love reigns the impossible may be attained."

Indian Proverb

"Love is composed of a single soul inhabiting two bodies."

Aristotle

"I CAN LIVE WITHOUT MONEY, I CANNOT LIVE WITHOUT LOVE."

JUDY GARLAND

"Hatred paralyzes life; love releases it. Hatred confuses life; love harmonizes it. Hatred darkens life; love illumines it."

Martin Luther King, Jr.

"Give me a kiss, and to that kiss a score;
Then to that twenty, add a hundred more;
A Thousand to that hundred; so kiss on,
To make that thousand up a million,
Treble that million, and when that is one,
Let's kiss afresh, as when we first begun."

Robert Herrick

"You come to love not by finding the perfect person, but by seeing an imperfect person perfectly."

Sam Keen

"WHEN I FIRST MET YOU, I WAS AFRAID TO TALK TO YOU. WHEN I TALKED TO YOU, I WAS AFRAID TO KISS YOU. WHEN I KISSED YOU, I WAS AFRAID TO LOVE YOU. NOW THAT I LOVE YOU, I'M AFRAID TO LOSE YOU."

KUUIPO MARK

"Life is the first gift, love is the second."

Marge Piercy

"To be able to say how much love, is love but little."

Petrarch

"The madness of love is the greatest of Heaven's blessings."

Plato

"The minute I heard my first
love story, I started looking for you,
Not knowing how blind that was.
Lovers don't finally meet somewhere,
They're in each other all along."

Rumi

"TWO PERSONS WHO LOVE
EACH OTHER ARE IN A PLACE
MORE HOLY THAN THE
INTERIOR OF A CHURCH."

WILLIAM LYON PHELPS

"LOVE IS THE ONLY GOLD."
ALFRED, LORD TENNYSON

"It takes a second to notice someone,
An hour to like someone,
A day to fall in love with someone,
And a life time to forget them."

Brittney Shea

"I love you—I am at
rest with you—
I have come home."

Dorothy L. Sayers

"I want you for always—
days, years, eternities."

Franz Schubert

"There is only one happiness
in life, to love and be loved."

George Sands

"LOVE IS THE EMBLEM OF
ETERNITY; IT CONFOUNDS ALL
NOTION OF TIME; EFFACES
ALL MEMORY OF A BEGINNING,
ALL FEAR OF AN END."

GERMAINE DE STAEL

"WE ARE MOST ALIVE WHEN WE'RE IN LOVE. BEING DEEPLY LOVED BY SOMEONE GIVES YOU STRENGTH; LOVING SOMEONE DEEPLY GIVES YOU COURAGE."

LAO-TZU

"Love is the only rational act."

Morrie Schwarz

"We cannot do great things—only small things with great love."

Mother Teresa

"I HAVE FOUND THE PARADOX THAT IF I LOVE UNTIL IT HURTS, THEN THERE IS NO HURT, BUT ONLY MORE LOVE."

MOTHER TERESA

"There are no monuments dedicated to me and my name will soon be forgotten, but I've loved another with all my heart and soul, and to me, this has always been enough."

Nicholas Sparks

"I arise from dreams of thee,
In the first sweet sleep of night,
When the winds are breathing low,
And the stars are shining bright."

Percy Bysshe Shelley

"The day will come when, after harnessing space, the winds, the tides, and gravitation, we shall harness for God the energies of love. And on that day, for the second time in the history of the world, we shall have discovered fire."

Pierre Teilhard de Chardin

"I am my beloved's and my beloved is mine."

The Shulamite

"WHAT IS LIFE WITHOUT THE RADIANCE OF LOVE?"

JOHANN CHRISTOPH FRIEDRICH VON SCHILLER

"It is best to love wisely, no doubt; but to love foolishly is better than not to be able to love at all."

William Thackeray

"To love and be loved is to feel the sun from both sides."

David Viscott

"IF I HAD NEVER MET HIM, I WOULD HAVE DREAMED HIM INTO BEING."

ANZIA YEZIERSKA

"LOVE ISN'T DECENT.
LOVE IS GLORIOUS
AND SHAMELESS."
ELIZABETH VON ARNIM

"Love lights more
fires than hate
can extinguish."
Ella Wheeler-Wilcox

"Once in a while, right in the middle of an
ordinary life, love gives us a fairy tale."

Gieselle C. Viera

153

"Love, love, love, that is the soul of genius."

Mozart

"This is the true measure of love: When we believe that we alone can love, that no one could ever have loved so before us, and that no one will ever love in the same way after us."

Johann Wolfgang Van Goethe

"Joy is not in things; it is in us."
Richard Wagner

"THINK ABOUT IT, THERE MUST BE HIGHER LOVE, DOWN IN THE HEART OR HIDDEN IN THE STARS ABOVE, WITHOUT IT, LIFE IS A WASTED TIME."

STEVE WINWOOD

"Love many things, for therein lies the true strength, and whosoever loves much performs much, and can accomplish much, and what is done in love is done well."

Vincent van Gogh

> ## "We must love one another or die."
> ### W.H. Auden

> "You never lose by loving.
> You always lose by holding back. "
> #### Barbara De Angelis

> ## "The mystery of love is greater than the mystery of death."
> ### Anonymous

> Mightier far
> Than strength of nerve or sinew, or the sway,
> Of magic potent over sun and star,
> Is Love."
>
> #### William Wordsworth

"Love has nothing to do with what you are expecting to get—only with what you are expecting to give—which is everything."

Katharine Hepburn

"TO LOVE SOMEONE IS TO SEE A MIRACLE INVISIBLE TO OTHERS."

FRANÇOIS MAURIAC

"Love conquers all things; let us too surrender to love."

Virgil

"Here force failed my high fantasy; but my desire and will were moved already—like a wheel revolving uniformly—by the Love that moves the sun and the other stars."

Dante

"I AM, IN EVERY THOUGHT OF MY HEART, YOURS."
WOODROW WILSON

"The best portion of a good man's life, His little, nameless, unremembered acts, Of kindness and of love."

William Wordsworth

"To the world you may be one person, but to one person you may be the world."

Anonymous

When you fall in love, you'll be inspired.

Every love story echoes in Romeo & Juliet; listen to the music by Tchaikovsky and see if you can't hear yourselves there, too.

Do you feel like dancing when you're around them? Watch Fred Astaire and Ginger Rogers and trip the light fantastic together.

Don't expect each other to be perfect. That's not how love works. Love each other's imperfections—they're the things that make your partner unique.

MUSIC IS THE FOOD OF LOVE, SO TURN THE VOLUME UP.

Ice-cream, chocolate sauce, honey: do you really have any doubt that romance and food make perfect partners? "Like Water For Chocolate" by Laura Esquivel just proves that love is a feast for the soul.

Romance can blossom in the most unlikely places. Watch "The Breakfast Club," then go looking for your own mismatched misfit.

Ever felt like your lover was speaking a different language? Never fear: "The King and I" shows that when oriental splendor meets British reserve the results can be romantic.

You can't watch "From Here To Eternity" and not be tempted to recreate the famous kissing-in-the-surf scene.

MUSIC IS ABOUT BEING IN TUNE, BEING IN HARMONY, AND CREATING A GOOD RHYTHM. THERE ARE LESSONS TO BE LEARNT THERE.

Love song lyrics do make sense, they are true. Though only if you yourself are in love.

Scandal, corruption, seduction, revenge—and eventually redeeming love —are the subjects of "Les Liaisons Dangereuses" by Pierre Choderlos de Laclos. Could you reform a serial seducer? Or would you become the talk of Parisian society?

You find yourself defined by what you love.

To describe your most powerful feelings, soul music has all the right words. Aretha Franklin is the queen; "Say A Little Prayer" her crowning glory.

"Casablanca." Play it again ...and again ...and again . . . and consider if you could make the same sacrifice?

THE HEROINE IN THE OPERA "LA WALLY" GIVES UP EVERYTHING TO BE WITH THE ONE SHE LOVES. COULD YOU DO THE SAME? WHAT'S STOPPING YOU?

To capture for yourselves the heat and passion of a Spanish romance, listen to Rodrigo's "Concierto De Aranjuez."

Some love stories do get a happy ever after.

Search listings for showings of old romantic movie classics . . . then book two seats in the back row.

HOW LONG WOULD YOU WAIT FOR YOUR TRUE LOVE? FOREVER? MADAME BUTTERFLY, THE HEROINE OF PUCCINI'S OPERA, IS PREPARED TO DO JUST THAT.

HIT THE HIGH NOTES WITH SOME GOOD OLD-FASHIONED MUSICAL ROMANCE. PERFECT FOR AFTERNOON VIEWING WITH CHOCOLATE, TEA, AND EACH OTHER.

It's not just for Christmas: "It's A Wonderful Life" is a story about how love can make life worth living. And don't we all sometimes need to be reminded how lucky we are?

Summer is the perfect time for open air concerts or film screenings. Take a blanket, a picnic, and curl up together...

Storm clouds may gather, but remember what the song said. You can only face the music and dance.

"JE T'AIME...MOI NON PLUS" BY SERGE GAINSBOURG AND JANE RANKIN IS THE ORIGINAL SEXY SONG. YOU WON'T NEED ANYTHING ELSE TO GET YOU IN THE MOOD.

Could someone pick you up off the street and change your life? Well, it happened in "My Fair Lady."

Ever yearned for something more? The Bronte sisters did, living an isolated existence on the Yorkshire Moors. Charlotte gave us "Jane Eyre," a tale of timeless, enduring, and compassionate love . . .

. . . and from Emily's imagination came "Wuthering Heights." Read it and know great cruelty, great hatred—and great passion.

"Gone With The Wind": it's epic and enormous, and quite frankly we could all do with a bit of Rhett and Scarlett's passion in our lives.

Take your inspiration from "Sleepless in Seattle" and arrange to meet your lover at the top of the Empire State Building.

Love inspires us to ask questions of ourselves that otherwise we would never ask. What is worth putting ourselves on the line for? Love, of course.

For anyone who has ever dreamt of growing into a beautiful swan and catching the eye of their first love, "Sabrina" is another Audrey Hepburn star turn in which she does just that.

WHAT KIND OF ON-SCREEN CHEMISTRY WOULD YOU HAVE?

Find it impossible to be apart? Take inspiration from Elizabeth Taylor and Richard Burton: even divorce couldn't separate them.

We need
love stories
to survive.

Indulge your inner child and watch "Lady and the Tramp": silly, sentimental and, like love, will never go out of style.

ALWAYS BE READY FOR YOUR CLOSE UP.

Some moments will be so good, you'll want to write them down, to remember.

In the mood to remember
some summer lovin'?
Put "Grease" on and let
Sandy and Danny be
your soundtrack.

**TAKE SOME INSPIRATION AND WRITE
OR PAINT YOUR OWN TRIBUTE TO LOVE.**

In the opera "La Traviata," Violetta gives up her lover to save him from scandal and heartbreak. Could you do the same?

Planning a slow, insistent seduction? Try Ravel's "Bolero" on the stereo.

Sometimes, all you need is a classic: martini, little black dress, and seduction song. "Let's Get It On" by Marvin Gaye has to be the song.

Real life isn't always like a book; it can be better.

Watch "When Harry Met Sally" and fall in love with New York, with love...and with your best friend?

Real certainty only happens once. You'll know when it happens to you.

185

"Seven Brides for Seven Brothers" gives you seven love stories to enjoy.

Could you bear to be parted from the one you love? Read "Possession" by A.S. Byatt and see.

ROMANCE—IN FILM OR BOOKS—IS PROOF THAT NOTHING CAN SOUND TOO OVER THE TOP IF YOU SAY IT WITH ENOUGH CONVICTION.

Ever been to Rome? Plan to? Then you need to see "Roman Holiday": Audrey Hepburn, Gregory Peck and the perfect bittersweet romance.

Take some tips from Hollywood greats: they knew about dramatic entrances, the power of a single glance, and the importance of a strategic costume change.

When it's difficult to say goodbye, remember how lucky you are to love someone as much as that.

If only we all had scriptwriters; then it would be easy to tell each other how we feel.

Rock Hudson and Doris Day should be your models for flirty, silly seduction.

In the sweetest French film ever made, Amelie finally greets her soulmate with a gentle kiss; watch with your soulmate, then do the same.

ROMANCE CAN BE THE SWEEP OF AN OPERATIC OVERTURE, OR THE BRUSH OF FINGERS REACHING FOR THE POPCORN.

Are you arranging a meeting by moonlight? "The Moonlight Sonata" by Beethoven is soft, gentle, and tender. Hopefully, your encounter will be the same.

WRITE YOUR PARTNER A STORY, OF YOUR LIFE TOGETHER SO FAR, AND THE LIFE YOU HOPE TO SHARE WITH THEM.

BROKEN HEARTS, UNREQUITED PASSION, AND TRUE LOVE: OPERA AND POP MUSIC ALIKE WILL GIVE YOU IT ALL.

The characters in the opera "La Boheme" are penniless, but rich in love. Listen, and remember that the most precious thing in your life could not be bought.

Listen to "Take A Walk on the Wild Side" by Lou Reed and be inspired to take your lover for an outrageous adventure (even if you come home safe and sound at the end of the night).

For your next date, imagine yourself as a director and create the perfect scene, from music, to lighting, dialogue, and costume.

On the path from youth to old age you'll encounter several different versions of "you." How wonderful to share them all with the person you fell in love with.

If you have a taste for the exotic, you will love "The Far Pavillions" by M.M. Kaye: a tale of forbidden romance in India.

From the lightening-quick mind of an eighteenth-century spinster named Jane Austen came the most charming, witty, and seductive romances ever put to paper. Every woman wants to be Lizzy from "Pride and Prejudice;" with eyes beautiful enough to win her Darcy's heart . . .

. . . or, if you're the eternal single girl, perhaps you long to be like the heroine of "Emma," who finds her true love is her best friend . . .

... but what's your romantic style? Passionate and intense, or unspoken and deep? The two sisters in "Sense and Sensibility" try both. Which love story will have the happy ending?

HANDS UP WHO WANTED TO TRY POTTERY AFTER SEEING "GHOST?"

Do you dream of wild passion in the wilderness? Watch "Out of Africa" and indulge your fantasies of lion-watching with your lover.

WE DON'T ALWAYS LOVE SOMEONE BECAUSE OF THEIR QUALITIES. THEIR FOIBLES CAN BE JUST AS APPEALING.

"West Side Story" is "Romeo and Juliet" set in the slums of New York. Watch, and remember that in romance no divide is too wide.

Make "I love you" the last thing you say to someone at the end of the day.

ROMANCE DOESN'T HAVE TO BE RESERVED FOR THE BIG SCREEN.

Think explaining how you feel is hard? Try doing it without speaking. Watch the sweetest scene in "Love Actually" for inspiration.

To express something simple and beautiful for the one you love, play them Pachelbel's "Canon." It's a strong contender for the most romantic piece of music ever written.

LOVE ISN'T ONLY PASSION: IT'S FUN, COMPLEX, SILLY, AND SCANDALOUS. PERFECT INGREDIENTS FOR MOZART'S OPERA, "THE MARRIAGE OF FIGARO," AND PERFECT INGREDIENTS FOR YOUR OWN AFFAIR.

Nothing beats the thrill of a hot, sweaty encounter on the dancefloor with an exciting stranger; and nothing is better than Prince's "Gett Off" to get the message across.

Love doesn't always have a happy ending. "Tess of the D'Urbervilles" by Thomas Hardy is bleak, tragic, painful—and utterly romantic. Read it and remind yourself how lucky you are.

"An Affair To Remember" is how you'd like all your romances to be: sassy and funny to start off; with a romantic finale to have you sobbing into your hot chocolate.

Ever had that feeling that you want to dance down the street in a downpour? "Singin' in the Rain" puts it on film.

REMEMBER "DIRTY DANCING?" NEXT TIME YOU'RE ON HOLIDAY, SEE IF YOU CAN SET THE DANCEFLOOR ALIGHT IN THE SAME WAY.

Are you more sharp-tongued than sweet-talking? Follow in the footsteps of Spencer Tracy and Katherine Hepburn, who made some of the best films of all time together, and had a 27-year-long affair—wise-cracking all the way.

Think love doesn't belong in the kitchen? Watch the lobster cooking scene in "Annie Hall," think again, and invite your lover to join you while you rustle up their dinner.

REAL LIFE CAN BE AS GOOD AS THE MOVIES.

If you've ever longed for a knight on a white charger to ride into your life and take you away (not before ripping your bodice to bits), read "Katherine" by Anya Seyton. This Medieval romance has it all.

The end of a doomed affair can be as sexy and sultry as the start. Don't believe it? Listen to "Wicked Game" by Chris Isaak and think again.

Love can be cruel, tragic, and painful. The story of the opera "Lakmé," of a priestess who falls in love with her father's sworn enemy, proves that it is always worth it.

SOMETIMES ONLY A WEEPY WILL DO. IN WHICH CASE, CHOOSE "LOVE STORY." ONLY WATCH WITH A STRONG SHOULDER TO CRY ON.

You never stop loving someone, even when they're away from you. Especially when they're away from you.

BE YOUR OWN ROMANTIC HEROES.

Spiderman is famous for the upside-down kiss. But think about it: isn't your lover a superhero of sorts? Don't they deserve a little adventurous romance?

EVER FEEL LIKE YOUR LIFE IS A RIDDLE? THE CHARACTERS IN THE OPERA "TURANDOT" SEARCH FOR THE SOLUTION. THE ANSWER THEY FIND? LOVE, OF COURSE.

Are you in a rock'n'roll romance? Slightly crazy, a little bit dangerous and always sexy? Then you have to listen to "Need You Tonight" by INXS.

Could your life be turned upside down by passion? Read "Anna Karenina" by Leo Tolstoy and see that love can be devastating and destructive, too.

"Pretty Woman" is the perfect update of the Cinderella story; just right for anyone who believes that love will save them. It will, whether you're a working girl or a millionaire.

"PEOPLE DO FALL IN LOVE. PEOPLE DO BELONG TO EACH OTHER. BECAUSE THAT'S THE ONLY CHANCE ANYBODY'S GOT FOR REAL HAPPINESS."

"BREAKFAST AT TIFFANY'S"

Everything you create is made from love.

Ever felt haunted by a figure from your lover's past? Read "Rebecca" by Daphne Du Maurier and discover that ghosts—even in rambling houses on the remote Cornish coast— aren't always what they appear.

Ever felt tempted to test your lover's faithfulness? The handsome heroes of Mozart's opera "Cosi Fan Tutte" do just that. What results would you find?

Need a quick injection of romance in film form? "Romeo and Juliet," in any version, with any cast, will always fit the bill.

"I FEEL LOVE" BY DONNA SUMMER. FLASHING LIGHTS, BARE LIMBS, STEAMY HEAT, AND WRITHING BODIES. DISCO WAS NEVER SEXIER.

How long could you wait to be with the person you love? "Love in the Time of Cholera" by Gabriel Garcia Marquez shows that a lifetime isn't too long.

There's a reason romantic comedies are popular: nothing makes you fall in love like laughing.

COULD YOU, LIKE MEG RYAN IN "SLEEPLESS IN SEATTLE," FALL IN LOVE WITH SOMEONE YOU'VE ONLY HEARD ON THE RADIO? IN A FILM—AS IN LIFE—ANYTHING IS POSSIBLE.

When you find the right person you don't want to waste any time getting on with the rest of your life. Together.

Fancy giving someone a bit of a giggle, as well as getting the message across? No Seventies seduction was complete without "I'm Gonna Love You Just A Little Bit More" by Barry White. Don't forget the fondue.

WILD, SEXY, AND ABANDONED, CARMEN IS A THOROUGHLY MODERN OPERATIC HEROINE. PUT HER STORY ON THE STEREO, AND PREPARE TO HIT SOME HIGH NOTES YOURSELF.

Romance can happen when you're badly dressed, tired, and grumpy. But sometimes we want to read about it being decadent, sparkling, and glamorous: "The Great Gatsby" by F. Scott Fitzgerald.

Everyone has felt the romantic effect of warm summer sun, a sparkling blue sea, and endless time to get to know someone. Read it described in "Captain Corelli's Mandolin" by Louis de Bernieres.

WHEN LOVE AND LUST COMBINE YOU GET "FEVER" BY PEGGY LEE. LISTEN, AND AGREE: IT'S A LOVELY WAY TO BURN, INDEED.

If you're planning a Sunday afternoon curled up with your lover on the sofa, pick a sweeping epic of Russian passion to watch: "Dr. Zhivago."

SOMETIMES ALL YOU WANT IS AN INVOLVING, ROMANTIC SAGA TO LOSE YOURSELF IN. "THE THORN BIRDS" BY COLLEEN MCCULLOUGH IS PERFECT; MADE TO BE READ WITH THE RAIN LASHING DOWN OUTSIDE.

You don't have to be a world-famous author to find the right words to tell someone how you feel about them.

> # MEMORIZE LOVE POETRY; YOU NEVER KNOW WHEN IT MIGHT COME IN HANDY.

Were people more romantic in the past? Georgette Heyer would have you believe so; she's the queen of historical romance. If your life needs an injection of old-fashioned escapism, try "The Foundling": it's one of her best.

The English may not be passionate, but they're certainly romantic, as "Four Weddings and a Funeral" perfectly demonstrates. Fall in love with a Brit and find out for yourself.

Can a sweet romance survive a social whirl? And would you want it to, if you had a different party to go to every night? "Vile Bodies" by Evelyn Waugh tells the story of the bright young things of London in the 1920s.

WHAT WOULD YOU SAVE IF YOUR WORLD WAS SINKING? EACH OTHER? WATCH "TITANIC" FOR INSPIRATION.

What would you do to save your lover's life? Betray them? That's the agonizing decision facing Tosca in Puccini's opera.

Would your love survive war? Separation? Death? "The English Patient" by Michael Ondaatje tells the story of a romance that did.

People say "It only happens in the movies." But it doesn't. It could happen to you, too.

Watch a DVD together with the curtains drawn against the afternoon sun—your own private cinema.

Allow yourself to believe that romance is true.

Looking for a fairytale romance? While waiting, watch "The Princess Bride:" it features magic, miracles, true love, and the world's most perfect kiss. How could you resist?

WHEN THE CREDITS ROLL ON YOUR PERSONAL LOVE STORY, LEAVE THE AUDIENCE CHEERING FOR MORE.

223

What has inspired the greatest artists, writers, actors, directors ... and you? Love.

ROMANTIC FOOD AND DRINK

COCKTAIL: BRIEF ENCOUNTER

- *1 measure peach schnapps*
- *1 measure coconut liqueur*
- *1 scoop orange sorbet*
- *Dash grenadine*

Blend the sorbet and alcohol until smooth. Decant into a tall glass and drizzle with the grenadine.

"The torch of love is lit in the kitchen."
French Proverb

For thousands of years, certain foods have been famous for inflaming the senses and fuelling passionate love. Try combining as many as you can in a meal—then enjoy the results.

Best restaurants: Petrinske Terasy Bar, Prague.
An outdoor terrace offers you spectacular panoramic
views over the romantic city of Prague.

GIVING YOUR VALENTINE A GIFT OF FOOD YOU'VE PREPARED YOURSELF IS ROMANTIC, THOUGHTFUL, AND SWEET: IN BOTH SENSES OF THE WORD!

COCKTAIL: WHITE HEART

- $\frac{1}{2}$ measure sambuca
- $\frac{1}{2}$ measure white crème de cacao
- 2 measures cream

  Shake with ice and strain into a cocktail glass.

ONIONS MIGHT BE A SURPRISING APHRODISIAC, BUT WHO ARE WE TO ARGUE? COOK UP SOME DELICIOUS SOUP FOR YOUR OTHER HALF.

ROMANTIC RECIPE: CASTILIAN HOT CHOCOLATE

- Mix 2oz/55g of unsweetened cocoa and 6oz/200g of superfine granulated sugar together. Dissolve 1oz/25g of cornflour in 7 fl oz/200ml of water and combine it with the cocoa and sugar in a pan. Stir until it's a smooth paste. Begin to heat the mixture, continually stirring with a whisk. Add 1¾ pints/one liter of milk, a bit at a time. Continue stirring as you bring to a simmer. Simmer, stirring often, for ten minutes. It is ready when it thickens and is glossy and smooth.

All pine kernels are thought to be aphrodisiacs, but the pine nut with the most power grows only on the northwest side of the Himalayan mountains. Only for someone really special.

Asparagus is famed for its power to arouse.
Maybe because you normally eat it with your
fingers, butter dripping down your wrist . . .

COCKTAIL: ADONIS
- 1 MEASURE RED VERMOUTH
- 2 MEASURE SWEET SHERRY
- DASH ORANGE BITTERS
MIX AND SERVE OVER ICE.

There's nothing sexy
about being on a diet.

Oysters are perhaps the world's most famous aphrodisiac and are
perfect for old-fashioned seduction. Serve on ice, with attitude.

BEST RESTAURANTS: CHEZ ANGELINE, PARIS. THE BEST HOT CHOCOLATE EVER—THICK, SWEET, AND CREAMY.

Truffles are precious, delicious, and full of erotic properties.

ROMANTIC RECIPE
Buy a heartshaped cutter and give a box of these warmly spicy cookies.
Preheat the oven to 190°C. Beat together 5oz/125g brown sugar and 5oz/125g butter. Beat one egg in a separate bowl then add the egg bit by bit to the sugar and butter. Sift in 9oz/250g all-purpose flour, two tsps mixed spice and a pinch of salt and mix well until you have a firm ball of dough. On a floured surface, roll out to a quarter inch thickness, cut into hearts, and bake for 15 minutes.

FOR AL FRESCO DINING ON
A SULTRY SUMMER NIGHT

Seafood salad, fresh peaches still warm from the sun, lots of tequila until late into the night.

COCKTAIL: ENGLISH ROSE

- $1/2$ measure dry vermouth
- 1 measure gin
- $1/2$ measure apricot brandy
- $1/2$ tsp lemon juice
- 1 tsp grenadine
- Sugar

Rub the rim of the lemon juice and dip into the sugar. Shake the vermouth, gin, brandy, lemon juice, and grenadine with ice, and strain into the sugar-rimmed glass.

THE ANCIENT CHINESE CONSIDERED APRICOTS AND PEACHES TO BE A SYMBOL OF A SENSUAL NATURE. UNSURPRISING WHEN YOU CONSIDER THE SOFT, SWEET FLESH OF A RIPE FRUIT.

EATING ARTICHOKES WAS THOUGHT TO STIMULATE CARNAL APPETITES: CATHERINE DE MEDICI WAS CONSIDERED SCANDALOUS AT THE FRENCH COURT FOR EATING A GREAT MANY OF THEM.

Sometimes all you need is a tub of ice-cream and your imagination.

COCKTAIL: ANGEL'S KISS
- 3 measures Tia Maria
- 4 tbsps heavy cream
- Cocoa powder
  Pour the Tia Maria into small glasses. Carefully pour the cream into the glasses over the back of a teaspoon, so that it floats on the surface of the Tia Maria. Dust the cream with cocoa powder.

BEST RESTAURANTS: LE LOTUS, TAHITI.
A gourmet restaurant that happens to be
suspended over a sparkling blue lagoon.

FOR THE PLANNED-TO-PERFECTION MOST ROMANTIC NIGHT OF YOUR LIFE: STRAWBERRIES AND CHAMPAGNE.

Melt marshmallows over a barbeque or fire and try to avoid getting the sticky mess all over your face. When you fail, kiss it off each other.

FOR A "JUST BECAUSE" SUNDAY LUNCH: ROAST CHICKEN; ROAST POTATOES (THE WAY THEIR MUM MAKES); FRENCH WHITE WINE.

ROMANTIC RECIPE: CHOCOLATE SAUCE
... perfect for licking

Melt 3¹/₂oz/100g butter and 3¹/₂oz/100g dark chocolate in a saucepan. Add 11¹/₄oz/325g icing sugar, 12fl oz/350ml evaporated milk and half a tsp of salt and cook for 20–25 minutes over a medium heat. The mixture will slowly thicken. Add 1 tsp of vanilla extract and serve. The sauce will keep in the fridge, but it sets like fudge, so reheat it to melt it down again.

There is simply nothing nicer than sitting by the sea sipping something cold and watching the sun going down.

COCKTAIL: PINK GIN
* ANGOSTURA BITTERS
* GIN

ADD A SPLASH OF BITTERS TO ICE CUBES IN A GLASS AND SWIRL AROUND TO COAT AND COOL THE GLASS. DISCARD THE ICE AND POUR IN A GENEROUS MEASURE OF GIN. THE BITTERS SHOULD TURN THE GIN PINK.

Garlic? Oh yes, it has been regarded as an aphrodisiac by the Egyptians, Greeks, Romans, Chinese, and Japanese. Cook up a spicy Italian dish and see for yourself.

VIRGIN COCKTAIL: STRAWBERRY SWEETHEARTS

- *8oz/225g ripe strawberries*
- *1 ripe banana*
- *1 tbsp sugar*
- *7fl oz/200ml cold milk*
- *2 scoops vanilla ice-cream*
  Blend all the ingredients together. Serve in tall glasses, decorated with heart-shaped strawberry slices.

SAFFRON IS A PRECIOUS AND EXOTIC SPICE. EATING IT MAKES EROGENOUS ZONES EVEN MORE SENSITIVE TO THE TOUCH.

ROMANTIC RECIPE: BAKE A HEART-SHAPED SPONGE CAKE
Preheat the oven to 170°C.
Sieve 3½oz/100g self-rising flour and one
level tsp of baking powder into a large bowl. Add
two medium eggs, 3½oz/100g superfine granulated sugar,
3½oz/100g soft butter and half a tsp vanilla extract. Beat all
the ingredients together, scoop into a greased, heart-shaped
cake pan and bake for 30–35 minutes. Make double the
quantity for two cakes to sandwich together with icing.

Cooking well for someone is a sign of affection, of care, of love.

FOR CENTURIES, GINGER HAS BEEN USED THROUGHOUT ASIA AND INDIA AS A POWERFUL APHRODISIAC. IN EUROPE, MAIDENS BAKED AND ATE GINGERBREAD MEN, BELIEVING IT WOULD BRING THEM A HUSBAND.

The herb basil is used in mysterious and powerful voodoo love ceremonies in Haiti. Why not invent you own version?

Get animalistic with spare ribs or chicken wings. Discard cutlery; bite, tear, and lick.

COCKTAIL: AFTER EIGHT
- 1/3 SHOT GLASS CRÈME DE CACAO
- 1/3 SHOT GLASS CRÈME DE MENTHE
- 1/3 SHOT GLASS BAILEYS

CAREFULLY LAYER THE INGREDIENTS IN A COLD SHOT GLASS. THEN SIP AND ENJOY.

Soft, succulent dates are eaten in Iran to revive a person's sex life.

For Friday night when they've been working hard all week: Whatever your local takeaway delivers and a few bottles of beer.

FOR A SATURDAY NIGHT WHEN THEY'VE RECOVERED: SPAGHETTI BOLOGNESE; CHOCOLATE TART; LOTS OF RED WINE.

Strange but true: the smell of doughnuts has been proved to stimulate blood flow to a certain crucial part of the male anatomy.

COCKTAIL: HÉLÈNE DE TROIE

- $\frac{1}{5}$ GLASS CRÈME DE ROSES
- $\frac{4}{5}$ GLASS CHAMPAGNE

ADD THE CRÈME DE ROSES TO A CHAMPAGNE FLUTE THEN TOP UP WITH CHAMPAGNE.

BEST RESTAURANTS: HAKKASAN, LONDON, UK. *Sexy and seductive subterranean restaurant with a never-ending stream of celebrity clientèle and fantastic cocktails—all with an exotic Oriental feel.*

Feed each other grapes and pretend you're at a Roman orgy.

Middle Eastern royalty used to use carrots to seduce potential lovers—because of their sweet flavor, or so their lovers could see in the dark...?

VIRGIN COCKTAIL: ANGEL PUNCH

- $3\frac{1}{2}$ pints/2 liters white grape juice
- $1\frac{3}{4}$ pints/1 liter cooled green tea
- $17\frac{1}{2}$ fl oz/500ml lemon juice
- $8\frac{3}{4}$ fl oz/250ml sugar syrup
- 2 bottles of chilled soda

Mix together all the ingredients apart from the soda. Chill.

Pour into a punch bowl with lots of ice and add the soda.

CELERY, BORING? THINK AGAIN. IT IS RICH IN HORMONES THAT STIMULATE DESIRE.

STRAWBERRIES ARE A CLASSIC SEDUCTION FOOD, BUT ONLY SERVE THEM IF THEY'RE IN SEASON, PLUMP, RIPE, AND LUSCIOUS. TRY THEM WITH CREAM, SUGAR, MELTED CHOCOLATE ... OR CHAMPAGNE.

BEST RESTAURANTS: LE MANOIR AUX QUAT'SAISONS, NEAR OXFORD, ENGLAND. Fabulous food served in a restaurant housed in an exquisite Cotswold manor house.

COCKTAIL: LOVE BIRDS
- **$1^1/_2$ MEASURES VODKA**
- **2 MEASURES SOUR MIX**
- **DASH DARK RUM**
- **$^1/_2$ MEASURE GRENADINE**
  MIX IN A GLASS. GARNISH WITH A CHERRY.

THE CLOVE SPICE HAS ENJOYED A REPUTATION AS ONE OF THE WORLD'S MOST POWERFUL LOVE FOODS SINCE IT WAS FIRST USED BY THE ROMANS.

The kitchen is the heart of the house.

Don't save best for special occasions. Tuesday night is enough of an excuse to open the expensive wine.

Eggs of all kinds—from quail's to caviar—are aphrodisiacs.

COCKTAIL: HONEYMOON

- **1 measure apple brandy**
- **1 measure Benedictine**
- **1 tsp Triple Sec**
- **Juice of ¹/₂ lemon**
  **Shake with ice and strain into
  a cocktail glass.**

For breakfast in bed, the morning after
a big night before: bacon sandwiches.

FOR BREAKFAST IN BED, AFTER THE FIRST NIGHT YOU SPEND TOGETHER: CROISSANTS; ORANGE JUICE; FRESH COFFEE.

FOR BREAKFAST IN BED, ON THE
MORNING OF YOUR ANNIVERSARY:
Brioche; butter; Bucks Fizz.

**BEST RESTAURANTS: CAPTAIN LINNELL
HOUSE, CAPE COD, USA.
A CHARMING VICTORIAN HOUSE,
DECKED IN TRAILING WISTERIA, AND
SURROUNDED BY ROLLING LAWNS.**

COCKTAIL: PASSION
- *1 large measure coconut rum*
- *1 large measure white rum*
- *1 tsp sugar*
- *Sours*
- *Pineapple juice*
- *Splash of lemonade*

Shake the rums, sours, and sugar and strain over ice. Top up with equal measures of pineapple and lemonade.

Fennel increases female sexual desire.
Try it on pasta, in salad . . . but try it!

ROMANTIC RECIPE: CHOCOLATE CORNFLAKE CAKE
- MELT 3½OZ/100G DARK CHOCOLATE WITH 1¾OZ/50G BUTTER, 1 TBSP OF LIGHT CORN SYRUP AND ONE TBSP OF POWDERED COCOA DRINK OVER A LOW HEAT. STIR UNTIL SMOOTH THEN STIR IN 4½OZ/125G CORNFLAKES OR RICE CRISPIES. STIR WELL THEN SPOON THE MIXTURE INTO ABOUT 15 BUN CASES AND REFRIGERATE TO SET.

SOMETIMES THE SEXIEST, MOST SENSUOUS FOOD YOU CAN SERVE ARE SIMPLE THINGS YOU CAN EAT WITH YOUR FINGERS.

COCKTAIL: WILD AT HEART

- $1\frac{1}{2}$ measures Irish whiskey
- $1\frac{1}{2}$ tsp grenadine
- $\frac{1}{2}$ measure lime juice
- Soda

  Fill a glass with ice, add whiskey, grenadine, and lime juice. Stir. Add soda to taste.

FOR WHEN THEY'RE FEELING ILL AND YOU'RE LOOKING AFTER THEM: *Chicken soup, hot honey and lemon to drink.*

THE EXTREMELY RICH AND EXPENSIVE GOOSE OR DUCK LIVER PATE, FOIE GRAS, WAS ONE OF CASANOVA'S FAVORITE SEDUCTION FOODS.

The Goddess of Love, Aphrodite, emerged from the waves in a sea shell. No wonder seafood is considered such a potent aphrodisiac.

Cocktail: Black Cosmopolitan
- $\frac{2}{3}$ glass Black label vodka
- $\frac{1}{3}$ glass cranberry juice
- Dash triple sec
- Squeeze of lime juice
  Mix and serve in a classic cocktail glass.
  Garnish with a curl of lime rind.

ROMANTIC RECIPE: THIS BUTTERCREAM ICING IS PERFECT FOR CAKES, TO EAT OFF THE SPOON ... or each other!

Add a few drops of red coloring to make it perfectly pink!

- Beat $4\frac{1}{2}$oz/125g butter until it's very soft. Gradually mix in 9oz/250g confectioner's sugar and then 2 tsps of boiling water. Mix well. Add food coloring if you like. Make sure your cake has cooled before you ice it, otherwise the icing will melt!

Sweet, spreadable, lickable honey is one of the world's favorite foods of love. The word "honeymoon" derives from the month that newly married couples spent together, during which they drank honey wine (mead).

IF YOU LET THEM HAVE THE LAST COOKIE, YOU KNOW YOU'RE IN LOVE.

The caffeine in coffee can increase alertness and arousal. Coffee drinkers are twice as likely to describe themselves as sexually active! Espresso, anyone?

COCKTAIL: CAIPIRINHA
- 4 tsp Turbinado sugar
- 1 measure cachaca
- 1 lime, cut into six segments

Add the lime segments and sugar to a stout glass and crush together with the end of a rolling pin or similar. Leave the lime in the glass and top with crushed ice. Add cachaca to finish.

BEST RESTAURANTS: 25TH FLOOR COCKTAIL BAR, SYDNEY, AUSTRALIA. The best views in the city, and that's saying something. This bar and restaurant has classic service and a menu to match.

COCKTAIL: BEAUTY ON THE BEACH

- **1 MEASURE WHITE RUM**
- **1 MEASURE SOUTHERN COMFORT**
- **1 TBSP GRAND MARNIER**
- **1 TSP LEMON JUICE**
- **2 DASHES ORANGE BITTERS**
  SHAKE WITH ICE AND POUR.

> *Mussels might not have the same reputation, but they pack a bigger aphrodisiacal punch than oysters.*

ROMANTIC RECIPE: CHOCOLATE MOUSSE

- Melt 6oz/200g bittersweet chocolate with 1 tsp of milk. Add $1\frac{3}{4}$oz/50g confectioner's sugar, $4\frac{1}{2}$oz/125g of butter, 5 egg yolks, and a pinch salt. Mix thoroughly. In another bowl, whisk the 5 egg whites until stiff and gently fold them in to the chocolate mixture. Pour into serving bowls. Leave to set in the fridge for at least four hours.

COCKTAIL: KIR ROYALE

- 2 measures crème de cassis
- Champagne
  Place the crème de cassis in a champagne flute and top up with champagne. Stir gently.

The chemical capsaican present in chilli peppers stimulates our nerve endings and makes our pulses race...

BEST RESTAURANTS: HARRY'S BAR, VENICE.
Right on the waterfront in the world's most romantic city, this bar invented the bellini cocktail; a divine mixture of white peach and Prosecco.

LICK YOUR FINGERS. THEN LICK THEIRS.

COCKTAIL: SINGAPORE SLING

- 2 measures gin
- 1 measure cherry brandy
- $\frac{1}{2}$ measure lemon juice
- Dash sugar syrup
- 3 drops angostura bitters
- Soda

Shake all the ingredients (except the soda water) with ice in a cocktail shaker. Strain and pour into a glass. Top up with soda.

VIRGIN COCKTAIL: HONEY LEMONADE
- 17FL OZ/500ML SODA WATER
- 8½FL OZ/125ML LEMON JUICE
- 2 TBSPS HONEY
  BLEND TOGETHER UNTIL SMOOTH

COCKTAIL: LOVERS' COCKTAIL
- 2 measures sloe gin
- 1 egg white
- 1 tsp lemon juice
- ½ tsp raspberry juice

Shake with ice and strain into a glass.

SHARE A HAMBURGER, LATE AT NIGHT, UNDER THE GLOW OF A STREETLAMP.

Figs are one of the sexiest foods on the planet, thanks to the way they split to reveal soft, fragrant flesh hidden within. Try feeding them to your lover drizzled with a little cream and a sprinkling of sugar.

ROMANTIC RECIPE: For someone with a real sweet tooth, tempt them with a tin of homemade fudge.

- ***Over a very low heat mix 14oz/400g confectioner's sugar, 9oz/250g butter, 3 tbsps of milk, 1 tbsp of vanilla extract, and a pinch of salt until the mixture is smooth and creamy. Pour into a greased 9"x5" tin and refrigerate until set. Cut into squares and deliver!***

Go food shopping together and turn a chore into a nice outing.

COCKTAIL: SEX ON THE BEACH

- 1 measure vodka
- 1 measure peach schnapps or Archers
- 7fl oz/200ml orange juice
- 7fl oz/200ml cranberry juice
- 2 measures raspberry syrup

Add all the ingredients to a glass, over ice.

ONE DESSERT; TWO FORKS.

**BEST RESTAURANTS:
PIL POUL, ATHENS, GREECE.
Beautiful and stylish couples
gather here to enjoy delicious
food and gaze on the stunning,
floodlit Acropolis.**

Sweet potato tarts were sought after in sixteenth-century Europe as a way to increase sexual desire... something to try?

Relive your childhoods with a packet of Oreos.

OFFER THEM A TREAT WHEN THEY'RE LEAST EXPECTING IT. A MOUTHFUL OF SOMETHING SWEET IS ALWAYS A NICE SURPRISE.

VIRGIN COCKTAIL: INNOCENT PASSION

- 4 fl oz/125ml passion fruit juice
- Dash cranberry juice
- Dash lemon juice
- Soda

   Mix in a tall glass filled with ice and top up
   with soda. Stir well and garnish with a cherry.

IF YOU FIND YOURSELVES AWAKE IN THE MIDDLE OF THE NIGHT, REMEMBER THAT NO ONE CAN TELL YOU OFF FOR HAVING A MIDNIGHT FEAST ANYMORE.

CHERRY FIX

- 1 measure brandy
- 2 measures lemon juice
- 1 measure kirsch

   Fill a glass a third full of crushed ice.
   Add the rest of the ingredients and
   mix with a spoon.

**FOR A SURPRISE WORKDAY PICNIC LUNCH:
A deli sandwich packed with goodies;
freshly made carrot cake; a smoothie.**

COCKTAIL: APPLE BLOSSOM
- 1 measure calvados
- $\frac{1}{4}$ oz grenadine
- Lemonade to taste
  Mix all the ingredients with ice. Strain into
  a tall glass filled with crushed ice.

Chocolate is perhaps the best-known
aphrodisiac. Scientists believe it induces the
same feeling as being in love, so share some
with your lover for a double whammy.

COCKTAIL: KISS IN THE DARK

- *1 measure cherry brandy*
- *1 measure dry vermouth*
- *1 measure gin*
  Stir with ice and strain into a cocktail glass.

ROMANTIC RECIPE: CHOCOLATE BROWNIES

Melt 9oz/250g bittersweet chocolate in a bowl over a pan of hot water. Mix 6 eggs and 9oz/250g sugar in a bowl. Add $4\frac{1}{2}$oz/125g almonds, $2\frac{3}{4}$oz/75g ground hazelnuts, $\frac{1}{4}$oz/15g vanilla sugar (or normal sugar), and the seeds from a vanilla bean. Then add $5\frac{1}{4}$oz/140g softened butter to the melted chocolate and combine well. Add to the rest of the ingredients. Pour into a greased and lined brownie pan and cook in a preheated oven at 150°C for about an hour.

Nuts have had a reputation as an aphrodisiac for centuries. During harvest festivals in Rome, maidens handed them out as fertility symbols. Why not do the same? (Dressing as a Roman maiden is optional.)

NUTMEG IS A FRAGRANT SPICE THAT HAS BEEN PRIZED BY THE GREEKS, ROMANS, ARABS, AND HINDUS AS A LOVE TONIC.

Some of your best conversations will happen when you're both stood by the stove, glasses in hands, with one of you idly stirring some pasta.

VIRGIN COCKTAIL: FUZZY LEMON FIZZ

- 7FL OZ/200ML PEACH NECTAR
- 5FL OZ/150ML LEMONADE
STIR OVER ICE IN A TALL GLASS.
SERVE WITH A LEMON TWIST.

For a surprise snack stop on a winter walk:
Ginger parkin cake and a flask of hot chocolate.

The Kama Sutra recommends the glistening red seeds of exotic pomegranate fruits as an erotic aid.

Elegant FLORENTINES make the perfect gift for a
sophisticated someone.

- Heat the oven to 180°C/350°F. Cover three or four baking
  trays with oiled greaseproof paper. Chop 1oz/25g glacé
  cherries and mix with 3½oz/100g cut mixed peel,
  1¾oz/50g slivered almonds, 3½oz/100g chopped
  almonds, and 1oz/25g golden raisins.

- Melt 3½oz/100g butter in a saucepan and add
  3½oz/100g sugar. Boil for one minute. Remove from the
  heat and stir in the fruit and nuts. Whip 2 tbsps heavy
  cream and fold into the mixture.

- Place small spoonfuls of the mixture on the baking trays,
  leaving them to spread. Bake for 8-10 minutes.
  Leave them to firm slightly before moving them to cooling
  racks. To finish, melt 3½oz/100g bittersweet chocolate
  in a bowl over a pan of hot water and use it to coat the
  underside of each florentine.

BEST RESTAURANTS: ELLEN'S STARDUST DINER, NEW YORK, USA
For classic 1950s American food.
Order up a milkshake with two straws.

Tequila, a strong spirit made from cactus, has been used for centuries in South America to promote sexual desire. Perfect, whether under a Latin sky, or in a cool cocktail bar.

THE QUINCE WAS DEDICATED TO APHRODITE AND VENUS. SOME THINK IT WAS THE FRUIT THAT TEMPTED EVE. TRY A LITTLE TEMPTING YOURSELF...

In ancient Arabic love manuals, pepper is described as a potent aphrodisiac for men. Spice things up a little.

COCKTAIL: FLIRTINI
- $1\frac{1}{2}$ large measures vodka
- 2 large measures raspberry vodka
- Cranberry juice to taste
  Mix together and serve over ice.

UNAGI, RAW SEA EEL, IS A POPULAR JAPANESE APHRODISIAC. LOOK FOR IT ON YOUR SUSHI MENU.

Anything can be made more enjoyable with the addition of some appropriately appetising food.

Vanilla is a powerful aphrodisiac, whether it's used as a scent or a flavoring. Sexy and sweet at the same time.

COCKTAIL: SHIRLEY TEMPLE

- 8 ice cubes
- 2 measures lemon juice
- $\frac{1}{2}$ measure grenadine
- $\frac{1}{2}$ measure sugar syrup
- Ginger ale

  Put the lemon juice, grenadine, and sugar syrup in a shaker with six ice cubes. Shake and strain into a glass and add the remaining ice. Top with ginger ale.

ALWAYS—ALWAYS—LEAVE THE DISHES UNTIL THE NEXT MORNING. YOU CAN SURELY THINK OF SOMETHING BETTER TO DO.

COCKTAIL: MINT JULEP
- 8 ice cubes
- 1 tsp sugar syrup
- 3 measures bourbon whiskey
- Mint leaves

  Put the mint leaves and sugar syrup into a small chilled glass and mash with a teaspoon. Add crushed ice to fill the glass, then add the bourbon.

Walnuts have been used in France and Italy to intensify desire.

"ONE CANNOT LOVE WELL IF ONE HAS NOT DINED WELL."
VIRGINIA WOOLF

TV fan? Arrange a trip to see their favorite TV show being taped. This might mean hopping on a bus to the nearest TV studio, or a trip halfway around the world.

Ride the Orient Express to Istanbul. Curl up together and watch Europe slipping past your window.

RECREATE YOUR FIRST DATE: SAME LOCATION, SAME OUTFITS—SAME BUTTERFLIES.

FLICKING PAINT AT EACH OTHER THEN SHARING A BEER AS YOU ADMIRE YOUR HARD WORK IS SURPRISINGLY ROMANTIC—SO DECORATE A ROOM TOGETHER.

The Taj Mahal was built by the broken-hearted Shah Jehan to commemorate his beloved wife Mumtaz Mahal after her death in 1630. One of the world's most beautiful buildings and a monument to love itself.

If you can't meet in real life, log on and meet in the eternal twinkling darkness of cyber space.

If you're dating a theater fan, get seats in a box for the next play you go to see. That way you can be alone together, even in a huge audience.

Arrange a treasure hunt—around your town or round the garden. The prize: You!

Go on, be naughty, and call in sick to work, then spend the day in bed together. (Well, you are ill, remember.)

WANDER ROUND THE ART GALLERY TOGETHER. ENJOY THE ART, OR LAUGH AT THE ODD EXPRESSIONS THEY PULLED IN EIGHTEENTH-CENTURY PORTRAITS.

Do you dare? Try a parachute jump together. If you can face that, you don't need to be afraid of anything.

Full house?
Go to bingo and see . . .

Any excuse to get cosy: Find the goriest horror film you can, and enjoy clinging to each other in terror.

THE MOST BEAUTIFUL SIGHT IN AFRICA: THE ANIMALS MIGRATING OVER THE MASAI MARA. TAKE A TRIP OF A LIFETIME AND WATCH.

WAIT FOR THE NIGHT BUS TOGETHER AND COUNT THE STARS WHILE YOU'RE DOING IT.

You don't need an excuse for a lunch date. Meet at a halfway point between your offices. Bring your own sandwiches and feed the crumbs to the birds. Consider how much nicer this is than eating in front of your computer.

Feeling adventurous? Get on a bus together, just to see where it will take you.

EVEN IF YOU CAN'T TAKE IT HOME, GO TO A PET SHOP AND PICK OUT THE PERFECT PET FOR EACH OTHER.

Dinner at your local restaurant? Phone ahead and get them to lay your table with extra candles and flowers, and bring out a special dessert for your beloved.

On the back row, on the front row—or back stage. Get tickets for their favorite band.

Check into the Bellagio Hotel in Las Vegas. Admire the spectacular landmark fountains; try your luck on the tables; try to resist the lure of the wedding chapels . . .

WILL YOUR LUCK BE IN? HAVE A DAY AT THE RACES, DRINKING CHAMPAGNE AND WINNING—OR LOSING— MONEY ON THE HORSES.

Could there be a better venue for romance than Paris? Sit on the steps of the Sacré Coeur in Montmartre, eating croissants and enjoying your vantage point over the city.

Make like the movie and have breakfast at Tiffany's. Get coffee and pretzels and window shop at 6 a.m. Then walk up Fifth Avenue in the sunshine.

The London Eye in the evening is the perfect place to see the twinkling lights of the city laid out beneath you.

WANT A GUARANTEED WINTER WONDERLAND? FLY TO SOMEWHERE CHILLY FOR SNOWBALL FIGHTS, SLEIGH RIDES, AND WARMING UP IN FRONT OF A ROARING LOG FIRE.

Climb Uluru (aka Ayer's Rock) and watch it glow red in the light of the setting sun.

BOOK LUNCH SEVERAL MONTHS IN ADVANCE, AT THE COOLEST RESTAURANT YOU CAN THINK OF AND HAVE FUN CELEB-SPOTTING.

Can the two of you deal with life's ups and downs? Go on a roller coaster and find out.

Le Sirenuse, on Italy's stunning Almafi coast, is one of Italy's grandest hotels. It clings to precipitous cliffs above the sparkling Mediterranean and has long attracted celebrities and royalty.

RENDEZVOUS AT YOUR CITY'S TRENDIEST COCKTAIL BAR, AND DRESS FOR THE OCCASION...

... or buy your own cocktail supplies, a book of recipes, and host your own cocktail party for two in your front room.

THERE'S NOTHING LIKE SOME FRESH AIR TO GIVE YOU A GLOW. PULL ON YOUR BOOTS AND GO FOR A LONG WALK IN THE COUNTRY—YOU'LL BE ALONE FOR HOURS.

What is the Mona Lisa smiling about?
Roam the treasure-packed halls of the
Louvre in Paris and find out.

Do you know an adrenalin junkie who'd love to take a few high-speed circuits round a Grand Prix circuit? Arrange it for them and their pulse will quicken before they even get near the track.

STARGAZE FROM THE DESERT AND CONTEMPLATE INFINITY TOGETHER.

There's something so sweet about getting ever-so-slightly tipsy with your lover. Raucous singing along with the radio, ridiculous dancing and hysterics over your favorite comedy video are all heartily recommended.

Venice: the perfect place to get lost, taking in secluded courtyards, crumbling palazzos, and shady canals along the way.

If you horse ride,
go for a gentle hack
across country . . .

. . . if you don't ride, take a
lesson, and soothe each others'
saddle sores afterward.

FANCY A LITTLE FRIENDLY
COMPETITION? GO TO THE GYM
TOGETHER AND COMPETE ON
THE CROSS TRAINER. THE LOSER
HAS TO MAKE DINNER.

On a lazy, hazy summer day, pack up a picnic and head for the country—or the nearest park—for some al fresco dining . . .

. . . **but if the weather's not up to it, have a carpet picnic: finger food and strawberries while lounging on the floor. (Make sure you vacuum first.)**

Get dressed to impress, hit the biggest club in town, and dance until the sun comes up.

Soccer fan? Watch your team and hope for a few goals so you can do lots of celebratory hugging and jumping up and down.

FEEL LIKE ADDING SOME EXPLOSIVE PASSION TO YOUR LIFE? HIKE UP A VOLCANO AND FEEL THE HEAT.

Love is one of the most powerful forces in the world; experience another at Niagara Falls.

The Portobello Hotel is one of London's best boutique hotels, in the heart of hip Notting Hill. Each of the exquisite rooms is different; try the Round Bed Room, or the Moroccan Room for an Arabian night.

Any sunset, from any beach: It's about the most perfect date you could have . . .

... AND ONLY GETS BETTER IF YOU'RE STILL UP TO WATCH THE SUNRISE THE NEXT MORNING.

Go to the zoo and check out the animals. Bonus points if one of you ends up doing an impression of a monkey.

Surf's up! Learn to ride the waves together, whether it's in Cornwall or California.

DATES DON'T HAVE TO LAST FOR LONG. A FIVE-MINUTE PHONE CALL CAN LIFT YOUR DAY.

Who needs a crowd? Have a firework party for two, complete with a bonfire, sparklers, and big bangs. Too much fun to be kept for November.

Stormy weather needn't be a bad thing, so get caught in a rainstorm. If one of you lets the other shelter under their coat, it's true love. But in any case, a wet shirt can be rather fetching attire.

SPEND ALL AFTERNOON LAZING IN THE PARK. IF YOU'RE FEELING ACTIVE, THROW A FRISBEE AROUND FOR FIVE MINUTES, THEN LIE DOWN AGAIN.

Sunday papers. Chic pavement cafe. Intellectual conversations over latte.

If your other half can listen to you murdering "I Will Survive" and still love you, you know you're on to something special, so sing your hearts out at a karaoke bar.

One of the wonders of the world, go scuba diving at the Great Barrier Reef and explore the miraculous world hidden under the sparkling blue sea.

GO TO SEE A MUSICAL AND SING THE SONGS TO EACH OTHER ON THE BUS HOME.

If it's good enough for Romeo, it's good enough for you. Go to Verona and stand under Juliet's balcony.

Sun-warmed strawberries are perfect, sensual food. Go fruit picking together, and get some supplies to feed each other.

Do you have a way with words? Talk your way into the V.I.P. lounge of a bar and be treated like stars for the night.

Saturday night at the movies, without leaving the house. Provide popcorn, nachos, and a pile of DVDs, then dim the lights and enjoy.

In Paris, the George V Hotel sets the standard in traditional luxury. The Honeymoon Suite has three terraces from which you can see the Eiffel Tower and the city spread out beneath you.

Unless it's "Alien," take a trip together to the location of your all-time favorite film. Re-enact the love scenes while you're there.

IS IT TIME FOR A BLIND DATE—WITH EACH OTHER? MEET AT A BAR, PRETEND YOU'VE NEVER MET, FLIRT AND SEDUCE EACH OTHER ALL OVER AGAIN.

Awesome, inspiring, and utterly beautiful: hold hands on the edge of the Grand Canyon. Who else would you share it with but them?

Murder can be magic—at a murder mystery night, at least. They're funny and fun—and there's always an illicit thrill that you might be dating the murderer.

Walk the Great Wall of China,
or some of it, at least, and
watch the mist-shrouded hills
receding in every direction.

The Northern Lights are a spectacular light show across the northern sky. Head to the Arctic Circle and watch a display put on just for you.

WHO NEEDS A BED? CAMP
FOR A NIGHT TOGETHER;
WHETHER IT'S IN THE
MIDDLE OF NOWHERE,
OR YOUR OWN BACK YARD.

Everyone loves laughter lines. Get together at a comedy club.

A SUMMER OUTDOOR MUSIC FESTIVAL LETS YOU LIVE—OR RELIVE—YOUR ROCK'N'ROLL DREAMS.

Enjoy the best of English traditions and take afternoon tea at one of London's historic hotels. The Ritz offers cucumber sandwiches, scones, fruit cake, and pastries under a gilded ceiling, with exquisite service.

Devote an entire Saturday to shopping, brunching, and cab-hopping.

NEW YORK CITY'S "THE INN AT IRVING PLACE" IS A REFINED NINETEENTH-CENTURY HIDEAWAY, PACKED WITH ANTIQUES AND OLD-WORLD CHARM, WITH MANHATTAN WAITING JUST OUTSIDE THE DOOR.

GO SKIING. IF YOU CAN'T SKI, SO MUCH THE BETTER.

Want a really revealing date? Take each other on tours of your home towns and tell each other the stories of your childhood.

Hot thermal pools in Iceland are the perfect place for an outdoor bath.

The Golden Gate Bridge in San Francisco is one of the world's most impressive sights. Even more breathtaking when you see the sparkling blue Pacific flowing beneath it.

CARNIVAL IN RIO DE JANEIRO. DRINK CAIPRINHAS AND DANCE TO THE LATIN RHYTHM UNDER A SULTRY, STAR-STREWN SKY.

There's nothing better than heading to a beautiful hotel with the one you love, whether it's for a single night or for a fortnight.

UP, UP, AND AWAY ON YOUR VERY OWN HOT AIR BALLOON RIDE.

On an overnight train ride you can be rocked to sleep while cozying up in your fold-down bed.

The Lodge at Loch Lomond sits on the quiet shores of Scotland's most beautiful loch, with the majestic splendor of the Highlands all around you.

Take a day trip to the nearest beach. Make sandcastles and stroll hand-in-hand.

Fore! Play a round of miniature golf. No sulking if you lose, now.

BAKE COOKIES TOGETHER. IF YOU DON'T BOTH END UP COVERED IN FLOUR WITH MORE MIXTURE EATEN RAW THAN PUT IN THE OVEN, THEN YOU'RE NOT DOING IT RIGHT.

On a perfect summer afternoon, find a river bank; cool some wine in the current and let the water carry the afternoon away...

The thrill-seeking couple will love wet and wild white water rafting.

Need to warm things up a little? Build a fire, on a beach or in your garden. Then roast marshmallows and let the sparks fly.

Fancy a long open highway with nothing for miles around but each other? Take a road trip. A huge convertible is, of course, essential.

NOBODY CAN BE ANYTHING BUT DELICIOUSLY HAPPY ON A TRAMPOLINE—SO GO FOR A BOUNCE TOGETHER.

When you're on holiday somewhere you love, go house hunting. You won't buy anywhere, but you can dream.

At the Soneva Gili resort in the Maldives, the 44 suites and the luxurious spa are all suspended over clear blue water. Open-air bathrooms and sumptuous daybeds add to the air of utter indulgence.

TAKE A TRIP TO A STATELY HOME, AND BE LORD AND LADY OF THE MANOR FOR A DAY.

Hit the pool hall. Drink beers, squint through the smoke, and try to prowl around the table like pros (even if one of you doesn't know which end of the cue to point at the ball.)

Ball room, salsa, or swing. The dance doesn't matter, as long as you're doing it together.

323

Elegant, charming, and playful, a swim with dolphins is a memory to treasure. Treasure it together.

You're the grand prize in a Scrabble tournament.

There's still a child hidden inside. Hit the local play park and unleash it.

The Hotel Astoria in compelling St. Petersburg gives you the chance to explore the splendor of Russia's greatest city and sleep in beds covered in heavy Russian linen.

BATH TIME. CANDLES, SOFT MUSIC, BUBBLES, AND PLENTY OF HOT WATER ARE IN NO WAY OPTIONAL.

Time to unveil your inner auteur. Make a film together on your video camera and give each other roles, directions, and lines. You can have a première, too, though it's unlikely you'll want to invite anyone else.

The tourists always look like they're enjoying themselves so join them and go sightseeing in your own city.

CEMETERIES ARE PEACEFUL, CALM, AND STRANGELY ROMANTIC. TAKE A WALK AND WATCH THE BUTTERFLIES.

Brighton is England's original destination for a saucy weekend. The fresh and funky Hotel Pelirocco updates this fine tradition with 19 individually styled bedrooms. Try Betty's Boudoir or Absolut Love for a night you'll remember.

Be it a yacht in the sun, or a row boat at your local park, spend some time on a boat.

Go to a midnight showing at your local cinema...

...OR SKIP WORK AND GO IN THE MIDDLE OF THE AFTERNOON.

THE SWAYING PALMS, GENTLE BREEZES, AND LAPPING WATER OF HAWAII MAY BE A CLICHÉ; BUT REALLY, WHO CARES?

There's nothing like that delicious thrill of fear. Go on a ghost walk and hold hands when it gets spooky!

Whether you're feeling rich or poor, go window shopping at the most expensive jewelry store you can find. Try on everything you like—who's to know you can't afford it?

CLIMB A MOUNTAIN TOGETHER. A SMALL ONE, IF YOU LIKE.

If you're feeling brave, have tattoos done for one another. Something small, somewhere discreet, that only you two will know about.

An hour spent simply talking could be the best date of the year.

GO FOR A WALK ON AN EMPTY BEACH IN WINTER— THE POUNDING SURF AND SALT-BREEZE KISSES MAKE UP FOR THE COLD.

There are angels in the architecture of cathedrals. Go see if you can spot one.

THE PARADOR DE GRANADA IS PART OF THE INCREDIBLE MOORISH ALHAMBRA PALACE IN GRANADA, SPAIN. LET THE SCENT OF ORANGE BLOSSOM DRIFT OVER YOU AS YOU SOAK UP THE INCREDIBLE VIEWS. GRACE KELLY HONEYMOONED HERE, AND IF IT'S GOOD ENOUGH FOR HER...

Where is the tallest building you know? Climb it and enjoy the view.

In the autumn, go leaf-kicking on a Sunday afternoon.

A treat for a weekday night: stay in a hotel in your home city and have breakfast in bed before work the next day.

Buy canvas and paints and create portraits of one another.

NO MATTER WHERE YOU GO
WITH THE ONE YOU LOVE,
FEEL IT IN YOUR HEART.

LOVE THROUGH THE AGES

BE CAREFUL WHO YOU FALL IN LOVE WITH. NO MATTER HOW YOUNG YOU ARE—OR HOW OLD YOU GROW TO BE—YOU WON'T EVER FORGET THEM.

"Approach love and cooking with reckless abandon."

Sylvia, aged 77

LOVERS FROM HISTORY: NAPOLEON AND JOSEPHINE
The future Emperor of France fell passionately in love with the graceful, aristocratic Josephine after one meeting in 1795. He confessed he loved his wife to the point of madness.

"LOVE IS LIKE A LITTLE OLD WOMAN AND A LITTLE OLD MAN WHO ARE STILL FRIENDS EVEN AFTER THEY KNOW EACH OTHER SO WELL."

LAURA, AGED 9

Falling in love always makes you feel like a teenager...

...and, fortunately, love is the only excuse to act like one.

In ancient Greece, lovers would pray to Aphrodite, the most beautiful of the goddesses, who cared for and consoled those with unhappy hearts.

Amid the monuments of ancient Rome, the feverish festival of Lupercalia took place, and the youths of the city paired up to celebrate it—it gave us our own Valentine's Day.

Never underestimate the teenage delights of holding hands in the back row of the cinema.

"I lived for over 50 years with a good man. I think that's about as lucky as one person can be."

June, aged 87

"I THINK YOU'RE SUPPOSED TO GET SHOT WITH AN ARROW OR SOMETHING, BUT THE REST OF IT ISN'T MEANT TO BE SO PAINFUL."

MICHAEL, AGED 8

The innovative Victorians invented the kissing seat, in which you sit next to someone but facing in opposite directions. Thanks to its "S"-shaped back, it is perfect for romantic encounters.

"I knew I was in love with my girlfriend when we stayed up all night and I didn't mind that all we did was talk."

Jake, aged 15

"Love at first sight is easy to understand. It's when two people have been looking at each other for a lifetime that it becomes a miracle."

Amy Bloom

LOVERS FROM HISTORY: BONNIE AND CLYDE

The outlaw lovers from the Depression lived fast and died young in the steamy heat of the Deep South.

WHEN YOU LOOK BACK ON YOUR LIFE, WHAT WILL YOU REMEMBER?

YOU'RE NEVER TOO OLD TO GO ON A DATE.

"When I was younger I used to look forward to the day I'd have love figured out. Now I'm beginning to suspect I never will."

James, aged 82

SHARING YOUR LIFE WITH ONE PERSON IS GOOD; FAILING THAT, SHARING YOUR LIFE WITH LOTS OF GOOD PEOPLE WILL DO.

The Celtic goddess of love was named Branwen.

Growing old gracefully is overrated.

Handmade Valentine's cards were popular from the late fifteenth century—why not make your own?

"You are beautiful in your teens, you think other people are beautiful in your twenties, you feel beautiful in your thirties. In your forties, you realize it doesn't matter whether you're beautiful; it matters that you're you."

Adele, aged 69

YOUNG LOVE IS WONDERFUL— ESPECIALLY WHEN YOU REMEMBER IT IN YOUR OLD AGE.

LOVERS FROM HISTORY:
ANTHONY AND CLEOPATRA

The exotic Egyptian Queen was the lover of the handsome Roman Marc Anthony. They both killed themselves rather than live without the other.

> "LOVE IS WHEN YOU TELL A GUY YOU LIKE HIS SHIRT, THEN HE WEARS IT EVERYDAY."
>
> ABBY, AGED 7

"I don't know how it happened, but a few years ago boys were disgusting and now ... I love them!"

Emily, aged 15

EROS WAS THE GREEK GOD OF LOVE AND DESIRE. HE WAS MARRIED TO THE MORTAL PSYCHE, WHOM HE VISITED EVERY NIGHT, BUT SHE WAS FORBIDDEN TO LOOK AT HIS FACE.

YOU'RE NEVER TOO YOUNG TO FIND THE LOVE OF YOUR LIFE.

LOVERS FROM HISTORY:
ODYSSEUS AND PENELOPE

The Greek hero was separated from his wife for 20 years, including his epic ten-year quest to return to her, yet she remained faithful to him all that time.

When spending the rest of your life with just one person goes from being terrifying to thrilling, you've found the right person.

"The only thing
that feels different
about love at my
age is my knees."

Alfred, aged 92

"WHEN YOU LOVE SOMEBODY, YOUR EYELASHES GO UP AND DOWN AND LITTLE STARS COME OUT OF YOU."

ADAM, AGED 8

It gets harder to fall in love when you get older, so practice a lot when you're young.

> **"I've never felt more in love than on the day our baby was born. Now, we're not just lovers, we're family."**
>
> **Robin, aged 33**

LOVERS FROM HISTORY:
SAMSON AND DELILAH
The strongest man in the world was undone by his love for the beautiful temptress Delilah, who ultimately betrayed his love.

In medieval times, young men and women danced around the maypole on May Day, holding on to ribbons, hoping to become entwined with their lovers.

St. Dwynwen is the Welsh patron saint of lovers. Her lover was turned to ice by a magical drink and she gave up the chance of marriage to release him.

"DATING IS A GREAT FEELING, BUT FINDING THE RIGHT PERSON AND GIVING UP ON DATING IS EVEN BETTER."

JULIA, AGED 28

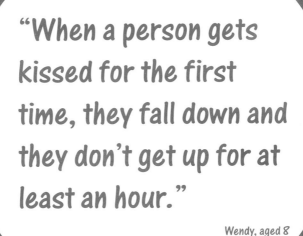

"When a person gets kissed for the first time, they fall down and they don't get up for at least an hour."

Wendy, aged 8

In the Norse mythology of Scandinavia, Freya was the goddess of love. In her beautiful palace, love songs were always played.

ENJOY COUNTING EACH OTHERS WRINKLES AS THEY GROW.

LOVERS FROM HISTORY: TSAR NICHOLAS AND EMPRESS ALEXANDRA OF RUSSIA

Despite their arranged marriage, the doomed rulers of Russia fell in love instantly and together endured rebellion, revolution, and death.

There is no harm in planning your future together; just don't forget the past, and remember to enjoy the present.

"To keep the heart unwrinkled, to be hopeful, kindly, cheerful, reverent—that is to triumph over old age."

Amos Bronson Alcott

AGE IS NOT A CURE FOR LOVE.

LOVERS FROM HISTORY:
ABELARD AND ELOISE
Abelard was a monastic teacher who fell in love with, and secretly married, one of his young students. After their enforced separation, their passionate affair continued in a secret correspondence of love letters.
They are buried together in Paris.

DON'T BE IN A RUSH. LIFE IS LONG; MAKE SURE YOU SPEND IT WITH THE RIGHT PERSON.

364

"If you start thinking, 'I can't believe I'm behaving like this. At my age!' That's a good thing."

Vi, aged 91

There's no rule that says you get better at being in love as you get older.

> "I've been out with four different boys, mostly for about two weeks each. The boy I really like, though, I'm too shy to talk to."
>
> Carly, aged 14

LOVERS FROM HISTORY: HENRY VIII AND ANNE BOLEYN

King Henry divorced his wife and changed the religion of England in order to marry his adored mistress, Anne. (Although a few years later he had her beheaded.)

Take comfort from the fact that everything you're feeling has been felt before.

"Don't waste your time worrying that you're not pretty enough, or you don't like him enough, or it might all go wrong. Love is too precious and life is too short."

Rita, aged 93

Don't worry too much about failed romances in your past: They're all leading up to the great success in your future.

At medieval courts, knights and ladies followed the rules of courtly love; writing anonymous love letters to each other and exchanging secret love tokens.

TAKE INSPIRATION AND ADVICE FROM HAPPY COUPLES WHO ARE OLDER THAN YOU—THEY KNOW SOMETHING THAT YOU MIGHT NOT.

You may think grand romantic gestures are old fashioned, but you are wrong.

"Age does not protect you from love, but love to some extent protects you from age."

Jeanne Moreau

There is no rule saying you have to meet the love of your life before a certain age. You might have to wait until your eighties, but you won't have to wait forever.

LOVERS FROM HISTORY: PERCY BYSSHE SHELLEY AND MARY SHELLEY

The pair met when Mary was just fifteen. She eloped with the poet two years later, despite the violent disapproval of both their parents and his wife!

Don't be cynical. No matter how old you are, or how jaded you feel, love is a miracle—regard it as such.

"When I look back, all the things I thought were important weren't really. The only thing that lasts is love."

Winnie, aged 86

A FACE ALIGHT WITH LOVE IS ALWAYS BEAUTIFUL.

"When my grandmother got arthritis, she couldn't bend over and paint her toenails anymore. So my grandfather does it for her all the time, even when his hands got arthritis too. That's love."

Sarah, aged 10

NO MATTER HOW LONG YOU'VE
BEEN WITH SOMEONE, NEVER
FORGET WHAT IT WAS LIKE WHEN
YOU FIRST MET THEM.

373

LOVERS FROM HISTORY: HELEN AND PARIS

Helen's legendary beauty caused Paris to fall in love with her, launched a thousand ships, and led to the Trojan wars.

> **"When someone loves you, the way they say your name is different. You know that your name is safe in their mouth."**
>
> **Ryan, aged 9**

When you meet someone when you're young and know you want them at your sixtieth birthday party, that's love.

"In my twenties love was intense and passionate. These days, things are calmer. I wouldn't have liked the idea then, but I actually prefer it. It's not so temperamental. I know it's going to last."

Adam, aged 42

NEVER GIVE UP.

Every holiday you take
in your life together
can be a honeymoon.

LOVERS FROM HISTORY: GEORGE III AND QUEEN CHARLOTTE

In an age of loveless marriages for power and money, that of the English king and queen was unique in being tender, affectionate, and genuinely loving. They had fifteen children together.

"Love seems the swiftest, but it is the slowest, of all growths. No man or woman really knows what perfect love is until they have been married a quarter of a century."

Mark Twain

"TRUE LOVE NEVER DIES FOR IT IS LUST THAT FADES AWAY. LOVE BONDS FOR A LIFETIME BUT LUST JUST PUSHES AWAY."

ALICIA BARNHART

"We come to love not by finding a perfect person, but by learning to see an imperfect person perfectly."

Anonymous

"Love is when you go out to eat and give somebody most of your French fries without making them give you any of theirs."

Tom, aged 6

There are as many different ways to love someone as there are days in your life.

LOVERS FROM HISTORY:
POCAHONTAS AND JOHN SMITH
Pocahontas was the daughter of a native American chief, who saved her beloved, a British settler, from execution by her father in the seventeenth century.

> **"Once you have loved someone, you'd do anything in the world for them... except love them again."**
>
> **Anonymous**

> "I thought I couldn't be more in love with my wife than on the day I married her, but I can honestly say it has grown every day. I doubt now that it will ever stop."
>
> George, aged 74

"IT TAKES ONLY A MINUTE TO GET A CRUSH ON SOMEONE, AN HOUR TO LIKE SOMEONE, AND A DAY TO LOVE SOMEONE, BUT IT TAKES A LIFETIME TO FORGET SOMEONE."

ANONYMOUS

"Young love is from the earth, and late love is from heaven."

Turkish Proverb

"LOVE IS WHAT MAKES YOU SMILE WHEN YOU'RE TIRED."

RACHEL, AGED 7

LOVERS FROM HISTORY: EDWARD VIII AND MRS SIMPSON

King Edward VIII reigned for just eleven months. He gave up the throne of England to marry Wallis Simpson, and as a result endured exile and condemnation for the rest of his life.

385

"First love is dangerous only when it is also the last."

Branislav Nusic

"When you're young you think you're entitled to fall in love; as you get older you realize you're incredibly fortunate if you do."

Julie, aged 57

Take your time falling in love; you only get to do it once, and this might be the last time.

"THOSE WHO LOVE DEEPLY NEVER GROW OLD; THEY MAY DIE OF OLD AGE, BUT THEY DIE YOUNG."

SIR ARTHUR PINERO

"The most wonderful thing about growing old with someone is that you go to bed with your lover and wake up with your best friend."

Laurence, aged 80

DEVOTE YOUR TIME AND EFFORT TO LOVE; IT WILL BE YOUR LIFE'S MOST IMPORTANT WORK.

"When you fall in love for the first time, the most incredible thing is how it's just as good as you thought it would be."

Polly, aged 23

LOVERS FROM HISTORY: MADAME DE POMPADOUR AND KING LOUIS XV OF FRANCE

The love of the King's life, the charming and witty Madame de Pompadour devoted herself to him at the decadent court of Versailles.

In days gone by, illicit lovers in Scandinavia would pray to Lofn, the goddess of secret love.

"Love is when my mommy makes coffee for my daddy and she takes a sip before giving it to him, to make sure the taste is OK."

Kate, aged 9

TEENAGERS LOOK FORWARD TO DATES FOR WEEKS—WHY STOP?

Look forward to the day when you've been together so long you can agree it's time to leave the party without having to say anything.

The Romans looked to Venus to assist their love affairs. The sensual goddess counted the gods Mars and Vulcan among her many lovers.

"TO HAVE BEEN WITH SOMEONE FOR THIS LONG, TO KNOW THEM THAT WELL, TO BE KNOWN THAT WELL; IT'S RATHER WONDERFUL."

ROBERT, AGED 67

"Infantile love follows the principle: 'I love because I am loved.'

Mature love follows the principle: 'I am loved because I love.'

Immature love says: 'I love you because I need you.'

Mature love says: "I need you because I love you.' "

Erich Fromm

"When I stopped worrying about trying to impress other people, that's when I found someone who was impressed with me."

FRANCIS, AGED 43

IN THE MIDST OF JOB, FAMILY, AND HOME, MAKE TIME FOR EACH OTHER. WOULD YOU ENJOY THE REST OF IT, IF THEY WEREN'T THERE?

Experience is sometimes worth more than enthusiasm . . .

. . . AND SOMETIMES NOT.

"Love is what's in the room with you at Christmas if you stop opening presents and listen."

Dean, aged 8

REMEMBER BEING A TEENAGER AND KISSING FOR HOURS? REMIND YOURSELF.

The story of Don Juan—the world's greatest lover—has been enjoyed for centuries. But despite his hundreds of conquests, he came to an unhappy end when a father took revenge for Don Juan's poor treatment of his daughter.

LOVE CAN LAST A LIFETIME.

"When you tell someone something bad about yourself and you're scared they won't love you anymore. But then you get surprised because not only do they still love you, they love you even more."

Robert, aged 10

LOVERS FROM HISTORY: CHARLES II AND NELL GWYN

The glamorous king of England had many lovers—lower-class Nell was the most charming and the most beloved.

YOU KNOW THE OLD COUPLES WHO STILL HOLD HANDS? THAT'S WHAT YOU'RE AIMING FOR.

"In the middle of family life, all that chaos, it's sometimes hard to remember why we fell in love. Then sometimes I just catch a glimpse of something in his eyes and it's like we're teenagers again."

Veronica, aged 47

Before there were phones and e-mail, lovers wrote letters.

Amorous Aztecs worshipped Xochiquetzal, the goddess of love. Every eight years a huge feast was held in her honor to celebrate with excess and indulgence.

If you knew when you were young what you know when you are old... you would do it all the same anyway.

LOVE LIKE EVERY DAY MIGHT BE YOUR LAST CHANCE.

LOVERS FROM HISTORY: TRISTAN AND ISOLDE
In the famous medieval romance, the prince Tristan falls in love with his uncle's bride, Isolde, as he sails with her across the Irish sea, to bring her to her wedding.

"You really shouldn't say 'I love you' unless you mean it. But if you mean it, you should say it a lot. People forget, and it's good for them to get reminded."

Sophie, aged 7

A HEART
THAT LOVES IS
ALWAYS YOUNG.
GREEK PROVERB

400

FINAL THOUGHT

"LOVE DOESN'T JUST SIT THERE LIKE A STONE; IT HAS TO BE MADE, LIKE BREAD, REMADE ALL THE TIME, MADE NEW."

URSULA K. LE GUIN

No matter how hard things get, is it harder than living without them?

Remember that to love someone is to wish them the best—not necessarily what is best for you.

On the days you don't like each other, remember you love each other.

Doing the washing up can make a lot of difference.

MAKE THEM A CUP OF COFFEE. FOR NO REASON.

FOR A RELATIONSHIP TO BE SUCCESSFUL, YOU NEED TO FALL IN LOVE MANY TIMES, WITH THE SAME PERSON.

Remembering anniversaries is the very least you can do . . .

...SO CELEBRATE THE ANNIVERSARY OF YOUR FIRST DATE...

...first kiss...

...FIRST TIME YOU ATE CHINESE FOOD TOGETHER...

. . . and anything else you can think of.

REMEMBER THAT YOU'RE IN LOVE. ACT LIKE IT!

If they've had a bad day, don't leap in with, "Oh yeah? Well, mine was worse." Just shut up and give them a hug.

"The hardest-learned lesson: that people have only their kind of love to give, not our kind."

Mignon McLaughlin

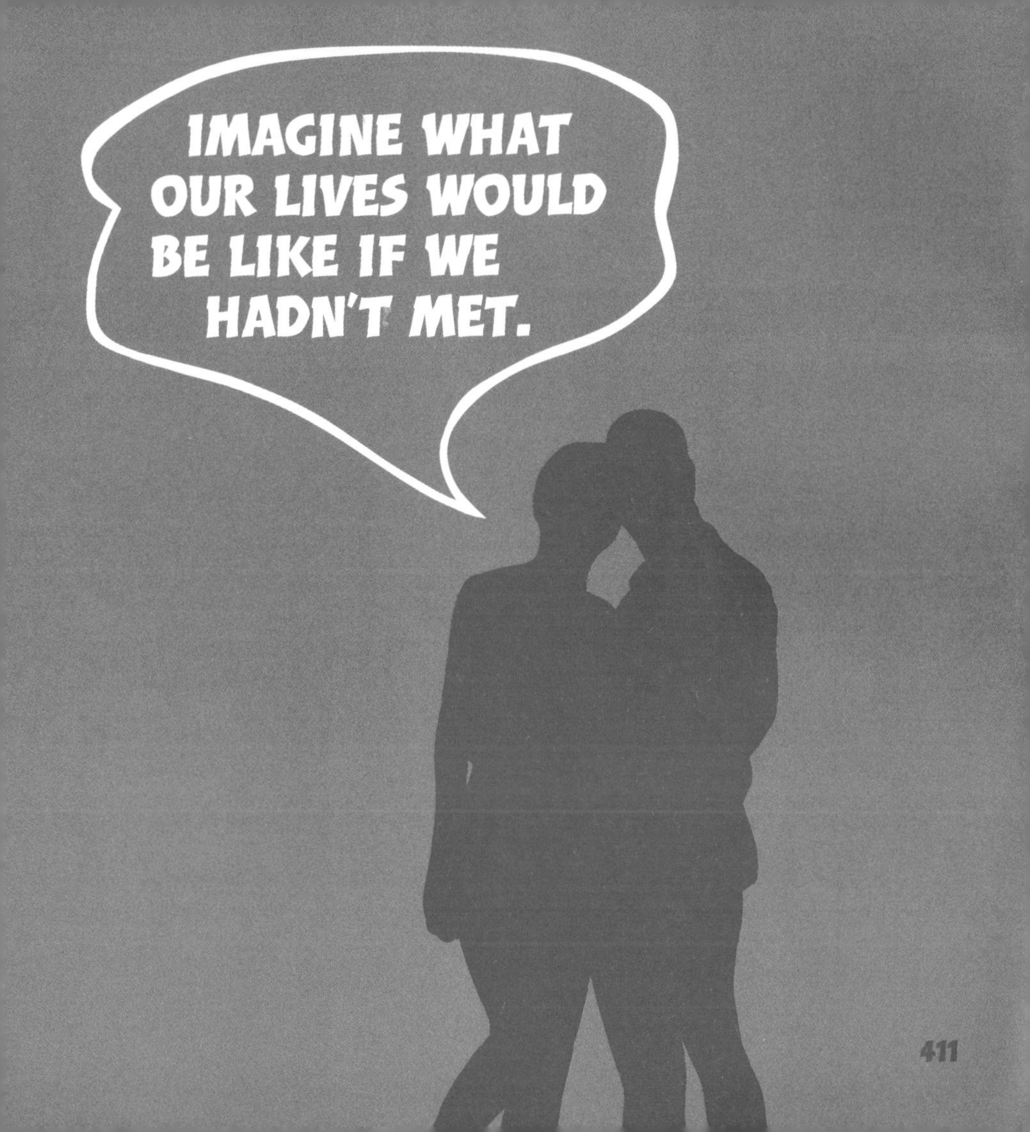
IMAGINE WHAT OUR LIVES WOULD BE LIKE IF WE HADN'T MET.

NEGLECT THE WHOLE WORLD RATHER THAN EACH OTHER.

First love is a storm; be thankful that you made it through to the calm and tranquility of your life together.

You can only truly communicate when you learn to listen to everything they're not saying.

PAY THEM A COMPLIMENT EVERY DAY.

And learn to be gracious when they compliment you back.

"Think not you can guide the course of love. For love, if it finds you worthy, shall guide your course."

Kahil Gibran

The only way to make love grow is to give more away.

TRY TO AVOID BEING ANGRY AT THE SAME TIME...

...OR AT LEAST IN THE SAME ROOM.

CELEBRATE YOUR DIFFERENCES.

"Love affairs are for emotional sprinters; the pleasures of love are for the emotional marathoners."

Robertson Davies

If you are too scared to lose someone, you might end up pushing them away.

416

Respect each other's right to an opinion, even if you don't agree with each other's ideas.

Don't shout unless the house is on fire . . .

. . . AND WHEN YOU ARGUE, WHISPER.

Dance with each other—
at a party or in the kitchen.

SEND A PRESENT, JUST BECAUSE.

Their jokes may be lame, but laugh at them anyway.

For your sanity's sake, take it in turns to hold the remote control.

YOU ARE NOT A MIND-READER: ASK THEM WHAT THEY ARE THINKING.

Together, you can survive anything.

FORGIVE EACH OTHER.

Early morning chats in bed are the best part of the day. Don't roll over and go back to sleep.

"Anyone can be passionate, but it takes real lovers to be silly."

Rose Franken

IF ONE PERSON LAUGHS, A FIGHT TENDS TO FIZZLE OUT.

Love means having to say you're sorry—even if you don't know what you've done.

TOTAL HONESTY IS NOT ALWAYS THE BEST POLICY.

A foot rub can make up for a million little annoyances.

"THE ENTIRE SUM OF EXISTENCE IS THE MAGIC OF BEING NEEDED BY JUST ONE PERSON."

VI PUTNAM

Apathy is more destructive than conflict. A fight shows you care.

Sometimes other things will come first—but remember to let them come second sometimes, too.

DON'T GO TO BED WITH AN ARGUMENT UNSETTLED. STAY UP AND FIGHT!

"A man reserves his true and deepest love not for the species of woman in whose company he finds himself electrified and enkindled, but for that one in whose company he may feel tenderly drowsy."
George Jean Nathan

Let them make it up to you.

You can only
be truly hurt
by someone you
truly love.

427

YOU PROBABLY THINK THEY KNOW YOU LOVE THEM. IT DOESN'T HURT TO REFRESH THEIR MEMORY.

Have a conversation with each other. You'd be surprised how much can change in the life of someone you live with.

Staring into the fire together on a winter's night can be as good as any conversation.

"Take love when it comes, and rejoice."

Carl Ewald

Whatever it is you normally talk about, make it a forbidden topic of conversation for one night.

TRY TO IMAGINE WHAT LIFE WOULD HAVE BEEN LIKE WITHOUT EACH OTHER. IT'S IMPOSSIBLE, ISN'T IT?

Take them a glass of wine when they're in the bath.

A KISS IS FREE AND PRECIOUS.

"Take each other for better or worse but not for granted."

Arlene Dahl

Never stop being interested in the person you're with.

There is a difference between hating something they've done and hating them. Make sure you know what it is.

COUNT YOUR BLESSINGS. MAKE THEM NUMBER ONE.

Put yourself in their shoes once in a while. It's always good to get a different take on a relationship.

Seduce them. You're probably on to a sure thing, but it doesn't hurt to make the effort.

You probably feel love more often than you voice it. Try to redress the balance.

Invite old friends round for dinner. I'm sure by now you each have a dish you can cook for them.

"Looking back, I have this to regret, that too often when I loved, I did not say so."
David Grayson

If you have to offer criticism, do it gently.

EVERY NOW AND AGAIN, WHEN THEY'RE NOT EXPECTING IT, MAKE THEM BREAKFAST.

MAKE A BIG DEAL OUT OF BIRTHDAYS.

Exclaim, "Oh my, you're so gorgeous" when they're wearing a new outfit.

Occasionally pretend not to notice that they haven't done their share of the chores.

Work hard on love. Everything else you have won't mean much without it.

WHEN YOU'RE WRONG, SAY YOU'RE SORRY . . .

. . . and when you're right, keep quiet about it.

And be big enough to admit that sometimes no one's in the wrong.

437

Drag them into the corner for a kiss.

Any day can be Valentine's Day,
and once a year isn't enough.

"The quarrels of lovers are like summer storms. Everything is more beautiful when they have passed."
Suzanne Necker

A sunset should never be viewed alone. Take your loved one outside and watch it together.

HAVE THEIR DINNER ON WHEN THEY GET HOME...

...or offer to go and pick up the takeaway.

HAVE THEY HAD A HARD WEEK? MAKE SURE YOU KNOW AND TRY TO MAKE THINGS BETTER.

They might be trying to tell you that they're sorry. They might not be using the right words.

There have been days when you couldn't imagine anything better than waking up with them every morning. Now you do, do you appreciate it as much?

Falling in love is easy. Being in love, that's a different story.

Do you have joint savings? Let them spend it on something you know they really want.

PRETEND YOU'VE FORGOTTEN YOUR ANNIVERSARY—AND MAKE UP FOR IT IN STYLE LATER ON.

Love is the answer; make sure you're asking the right questions.

Pillow fights aren't just for children . . .

...NEITHER ARE TICKLING CONTESTS.

"Yes" is a word you should use more than "No."

YOU LOVE EACH OTHER, YOU DON'T NEED TO BECOME EACH OTHER.

Don't always speak your mind; you might have changed it in the morning.

LUST FADES, SO YOU'D BETTER BE WITH SOMEONE WHO CAN STAND YOU.

Have they cut their hair?
Have they? If in doubt,
tell them it looks great.

"Treasure each other in the recognition that we do not know how long we shall have each other."

Joshua Liebman

Look through old photos and reminisce about your romance.

Patience isn't only a virtue, it's an absolute necessity.

WHEN YOU DON'T THINK YOU CAN LOVE THEM ANY MORE, TRY.

The TV? Turn it off. The internet? Unplug it. Make your own entertainment.

"It is not a lack of love, but a lack of friendship that makes unhappy marriages."

Friedrich Nietzsche

Your bedroom is just that; not a study, a storeroom or a playpen (except for the two of you).

GET DRESSED UP. BECAUSE THEY'RE WORTH IT.

Encourage them to dust off their best outfit, too. The two of you will cut quite a dash.

You are
writing
your own
love story.

You wouldn't expect a car to run smoothly without regular checks, so why would you expect love to?

If you are able to spend your life with the person you love, you're one of the lucky ones.

HAVE AN "OUR TUNE." AND LISTEN TO IT.

454

Schedule some time every week, be it an evening or an hour, to spend together. Don't let anything take priority over it.

"Nobody has ever measured, even poets, how much a heart can hold."

Zelda Fitzgerald

Put a lasagne in the fridge when you're going away for the weekend...

...AND DON'T FORGET TO CALL TO TELL THEM YOU'RE MISSING THEM.

Whatever effort you have to put in, it is worth it, and more.

Remember: For every annoying fault they have, you have one too.

TELL THEM THEY LOOK SEXY WHEN THEY'RE WEARING THEIR JOGGING BOTTOMS.

Make eye contact.

SOLVE ARGUMENTS WITH ARM WRESTLING, OR WATER FIGHTS.

If you're talking to them, don't interrupt them to answer your phone.

WATCH THEM DO SOMETHING THAT THEY'RE GOOD AT.

Be kind to one another.

THEY MIGHT NOT ALWAYS ACT LIKE
YOU'D WANT THEM TO...

...they might not even be capable of it...

...they'll be doing
the best they can.

"Love never dies a natural death. It dies because we don't know how to replenish its source. It dies of blindness and errors and betrayals. It dies of illness and wounds; it dies of weariness, of witherings, of tarnishings."

Anais Nin

DON'T HIDE IN LOVE. GO OUT INTO THE WORLD, KNOWING THAT LOVE WILL BE WAITING FOR YOU.

Ask them out on a date.

If one of you has to win the argument, let them.

IF YOU SAY, "IT'S UP TO YOU," MEAN IT.

"True love stories never have endings."

Richard Bach

Above all things, love one another.

Love can
last forever...